U.S. Fish and Wildlife Service

Waterfowl

Population Status, 2005

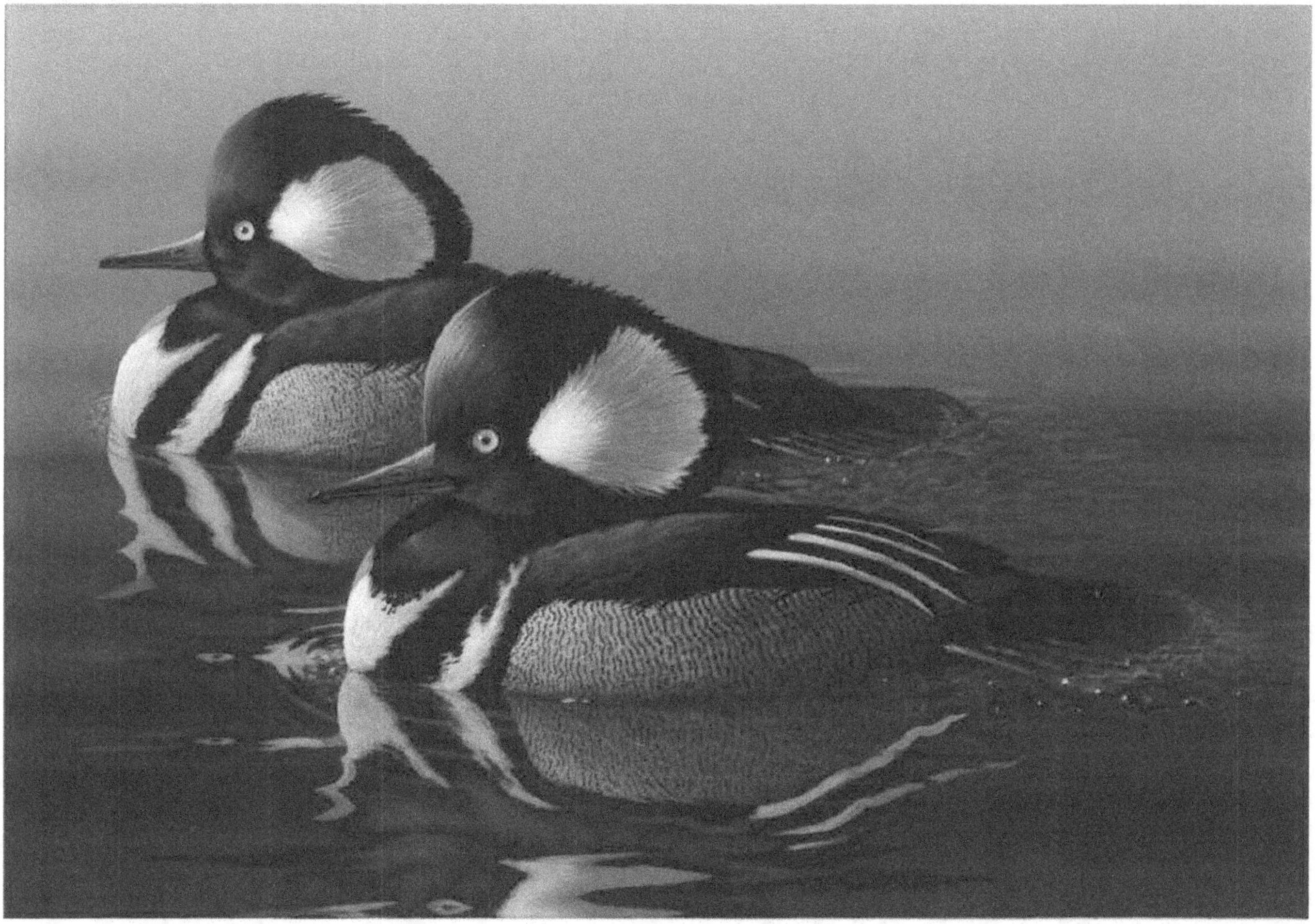

WATERFOWL POPULATION STATUS, 2005

July 25, 2005

In North America the process of establishing hunting regulations for waterfowl is conducted annually. In the United States the process involves a number of scheduled meetings in which information regarding the status of waterfowl is presented to individuals within the agencies responsible for setting hunting regulations. In addition the proposed regulations are published in the *Federal Register* to allow public comment. This report includes the most current breeding population and production information available for waterfowl in North America and is a result of cooperative efforts by the U.S. Fish and Wildlife Service (FWS), the Canadian Wildlife Service (CWS), various state and provincial conservation agencies, and private conservation organizations. This report is intended to aid the development of waterfowl harvest regulations in the United States for the 2005-2006 hunting season.

Cover art: Hooded mergansers. Mark Anderson winner of the 2005-2006 Federal Duck Stamp design competition.

ACKNOWLEDGMENTS

Waterfowl Population and Habitat Information: The information contained in this report is the result of the efforts of numerous individuals and organizations. Principal contributors include the Canadian Wildlife Service, U.S. Fish and Wildlife Service, state wildlife conservation agencies, provincial conservation agencies from Canada, and Direccion General de Conservacion Ecologica de los Recursos Naturales, Mexico. In addition, several conservation organizations, other state and federal agencies, universities, and private individuals provided information or cooperated in survey activities. Some habitat and weather information was taken from the NOAA/USDA Joint Agriculture Weather Facility (http://www.usda.gov/oce/waob/jawf/), Environment Canada (http://www1.tor.ec.gc.ca/ccrm/bulletin/), and Waterfowl Population Surveys reports (http://migratorybirds.fws.gov/reports/reports.html). Appendix A provides a list of individuals responsible for the collection and compilation of data for the Ducks section of this report. Appendix B provides a list of individuals who were primary contacts for information included in the Geese and Swans section. We apologize for any omission of individuals from these lists, and thank all participants for their contributions. Without this combined effort, a comprehensive assessment of waterfowl populations and habitat would not be possible.

Authors: This report was prepared by the U.S. Fish and Wildlife Service, Division of Migratory Bird Management, Branch of Surveys and Assessment. The principal authors are Pamela R. Garrettson, Timothy J. Moser, and Khristi Wilkins. The authors compiled information from the numerous sources to provide an assessment of the status of waterfowl populations.

Report Preparation: The preparation of this report involved substantial efforts on the part of many individuals. Support for the processing of data and publication was provided by Mark C. Otto, John Sauer and Judith P. Bladen. Ray Bentley, John Bidwell, Karen Bollinger, Elizabeth Huggins, Bruce Conant, Carl Ferguson, Rod King, Mark Koneff, Fred Roetker, John Solberg, Phil Thorpe, Dan Nieman, Dale Caswell, James Kelley, James Dubovsky, Robert Blohm, and James Wortham provided habitat narratives, reviewed portions of the report that addressed major breeding areas, and provided helpful comments.

This report should be cited as: U.S. Fish and Wildlife Service. 2005. Waterfowl population status, 2005. U.S. Department of the Interior, Washington, D.C. U.S.A.

All Division of Migratory Bird Management reports are available at our home page (http://migratorybirds.fws.gov).

WATERFOWL POPULATION SURVEYS

50 Years & Still Counting

This year is the 50th anniversary of the May Waterfowl Breeding Population and Habitat Survey.

Table of Contents

List of Duck Tables

List of Duck Figures

List of Goose and Swan Figures

STATUS OF DUCKS

Abstract: In the Waterfowl Breeding Population and Habitat Survey traditional survey area (strata 1-18, 20-50, and 75-77), the total duck population estimate was 31.7 ± 0.6 [SE] million birds, similar to last year's estimate of 32.2 ± 0.6 million birds but 5% below the 1955-2004 long-term average. Mallard (*Anas platyrhynchos*) abundance was 6.8 ± 0.3 million birds, which was 9% below last year's estimate of 7.4 ± 0.3 million birds and 10% below the long-term average. Blue-winged teal (*A. discors*) abundance was 4.6 ± 0.2 million birds, similar to last year's estimate of 4.1 ± 0.2 million birds, and the long-term average. Of the other duck species, the gadwall estimate (*A. strepera*; 2.2 ± 0.1 million) was 16% below that of 2004, while estimates of northern pintails (*A. acuta*; 2.6 ± 0.1 million; +17%) and northern shovelers (*A. clypeata*; 3.6 ± 0.2 million; +28%) were significantly above 2004 estimates. The estimate for northern shovelers was 67% above the long-term average for this species, as were estimates of gadwall (+30%) and green-winged teal (*A. crecca*; 2.2 ± 0.1 million; +16%). Northern pintails remained 38% below their long-term average despite this year's increase in abundance. Estimates of American wigeon (*A. americana*; 2.2 ± 0.1 million; -15%) and scaup (*Aythya affinis* and *A. marila* combined; 3.4 ± 0.2; -35%) also were below their respective long-term averages; the estimate for scaup was a record low. Abundances of redheads (*A. americana*) and canvasbacks (*A. valisineria*) were similar to last year's counts and long-term averages. The total May pond estimate (Prairie and Parkland Canada and the northcentral U.S. combined) was 5.4 ± 0.2 million ponds, which is 37% greater than last year's estimate of 3.9 ± 0.2 million ponds and 12% higher than the long-term average of 4.8 ± 0.1 million ponds. The 2005 pond estimate in Prairie and Parkland Canada was 3.9 ± 0.2 million. This was a 56% increase relative to last year's estimate of 2.5 ± 0.1 million ponds and 17% higher than the long-term average of 3.3 ± 0.3 million ponds. The 2005 pond estimate for the northcentral U.S. (1.5 ± 0.1 million) was similar to last year's estimate (Fig.1). The projected mallard fall flight index was 9.3 ± 0.1 million, similar to the 2004 estimate of 9.4 ± 0.1 million birds. The eastern survey area was restratified, and is now composed of strata 51-72. Mergansers (red-breasted [*Mergus serrator*], common [*M. merganser*], and hooded [*Lophodytes cucullatus*;], -25%), mallards (-36%), American black ducks (*A. rubripes*, -24%), and green-winged teal (-46%) were all below their 2004 estimates. Ring-necked ducks (*Aythya collaris*) and goldeneyes (common [*Bucephala clangula*] and Barrow's [*B. islandica*]) were similar to their 2004 estimates. No species in the eastern survey area differed from their long-term averages.

This section summarizes the most recent information about the status of North American duck populations and their habitats in order to facilitate development of harvest regulations in the U.S. The U.S. Fish and Wildlife Service and its partners conduct a variety of surveys to collect information on ducks. The annual status of these populations is assessed using databases resulting from these surveys, which include estimates of the size of breeding populations, production, and harvest. This report details abundance estimates and production outlooks; harvest survey results are discussed in separate reports. The data and analyses were the most current available when this report was written. Future analyses may yield slightly different results as databases are updated and new analytical procedures become available.

METHODS

Breeding Population and Habitat Survey

Federal, provincial, and state agencies conduct surveys each spring to estimate the size of breeding populations and to evaluate the condition of the habitats. These surveys are conducted using fixed-wing aircraft and helicopters, and cover over 2.0 million square miles that encompass principal breeding areas of North America. The traditional survey area (strata 1-18, 20-50, and 75-77) comprises parts of Alaska, Canada, and the northcentral U.S., and includes approximately 1.3 million square miles (Appendix C). The eastern survey area (strata 51-72) includes parts of Ontario, Quebec, Labrador, Newfoundland, Nova Scotia, Prince Edward Island, New Brunswick, New York, and Maine, covering an area of approximately 0.7 million square miles.

In Prairie and Parkland Canada and the northcentral U.S., aerial waterfowl counts are corrected annually for visibility bias by conducting ground counts. In the northern portions of the traditional survey area and the eastern survey area, duck estimates are adjusted using visibility correction factors derived from a comparison of airplane and helicopter counts. Annual estimates of duck abundance are available since 1955 for the traditional survey area and since 1996 for all strata (except 57 and 58) in the eastern survey area. However, portions of the eastern survey area have been surveyed since 1990. In the traditional survey area, estimates of pond abundance in Prairie and Parkland Canada are available since 1961 and in the northcentral U.S. since 1974. Several provinces and states also conduct breeding waterfowl surveys using various methods; some have survey designs that allow calculation of measures of precision for their estimates. Information about habitat conditions was supplied primarily by biologists working in the survey areas. However, much ancillary weather information was obtained from agricultural and weather internet sites (see references). Unless otherwise noted, the alpha level (P value) for determining statistical significance was set at 0.1; actual P values are given in tables along with wetland and waterfowl estimates.

Since 1990 the U.S. Fish and Wildlife Service (USFWS) has conducted aerial transect surveys using fixed-wing aircraft in eastern Canada and the northeast U.S., similar to those used in the mid-continent, for estimating waterfowl abundance. Additionally, the Canadian Wildlife Service (CWS) has conducted a helicopter-based aerial plot survey in core nesting areas of American black ducks in Ontario, Quebec, and the Atlantic Provinces. Historically, data from these surveys were analyzed separately, despite geographic overlap in survey coverage. In 2004, the USFWS and Canadian Wildlife Service (CWS) agreed to integrate the two surveys, produce composite estimates from both sets of survey data, and expand the geographic scope of the survey in eastern North America.

As a result, waterfowl population estimates for eastern North America will no longer be produced solely on the basis of USFWS-collected data, but will be based on both USFWS and CWS data. Estimates of populations in eastern North America (strata 51-72) in this report are composite estimates based on data from the CWS and USFWS surveys. For strata containing both CWS and USFWS data (51, 52, 63, 64, 66, and 68), visibility-adjusted USFWS data were combined with plot data; single survey results were used as the estimates for strata containing only one source of information (69, 53, 54, 55, 56, 62, 65, and 67 for transects; 70, 71, and 72 for plots). Strata 57 and 58 were not consistently surveyed over the interval 1999-2005, and were not included in population totals for the eastern area. Estimates for these 2 strata will be incorporated in future

reports. For widely-distributed species, (American black ducks, mallards, green-winged teal, merganser, ring-necked duck, and goldeneye), composite estimates of population size were constructed using a hierarchical model, in which change is modeled using a linear model that includes survey and transect/plot effects (e.g., Link and Sauer 2002). Area-weighted, exponentiated year effects (or averaged year effects, when both surveys were conducted in a stratum) were used as estimates of total indicated birds in each stratum (Royle et al. 2002). Additional technical issues must be resolved for species with patchy distributions in the eastern survey area (bufflehead [*B. albeola*], scoters [*Melanitta spp.*], American wigeon, and scaup); therefore estimates for these species are not presented in this report.

To produce a consistent index in the Eastern Survey Area for American black ducks, total indicated birds were calculated using the CWS method of scaling observed pairs. Observed black duck pairs were scaled by 1.5 rather than the 1.0 scaling traditionally applied by the USFWS. The CWS scaling is based on sex-specific observations collected during the CWS survey in eastern Canada which indicate that approximately 50% of black duck pair observations are actually 2 drakes. For other species, the standard USFWS definition of total indicated birds was used. Procedures for deriving composite estimates from surveys and defining total indicated birds are presently undergoing review and evaluation by CWS and USFWS personnel.

Another notable change relative to previous reports on waterfowl status in eastern North America is that estimates of population abundance are presented back only to 1999. Additional work must be done to reconstruct a composite time-series for the entire period of record for these surveys. Finally, we have taken initial steps toward re-stratification in eastern Canada (Fig. 1). Taken together, changes in indices, analytical procedures, geographic stratification, and the area sampled by the composite surveys mean that these revised survey results for eastern North America are not directly comparable with results presented in previous reports.

We anticipate other changes to survey design and analysis for eastern North America during the coming years, and view the composite estimates for strata 51 to 72 as the first step toward a fully integrated survey. They likely will change in the

6

near future as the USFWS and CWS agree upon the final survey design and analytical methods.

Production and Habitat Survey

For the past two years, we had no traditional July Production Survey to verify the early predictions of our biologists in the field, due to severe budget constraints within the migratory bird program. However, the pilot-biologists responsible for several survey areas (southern Alberta, southern Saskatchewan southern Manitoba, the Dakotas, and Montana) returned in early July for a brief flight over representative portions of their areas as a rough assessment of habitat changes since May and resultant duck production. This information, along with reports from local biologists in the field, helped us formulate our overall perspective on duck production this year.

Total Duck Species Composition

In the traditional survey area, our estimate of total ducks excludes scoters, eiders (*Somateria* and *Polysticta* spp.), long-tailed ducks (*Clangula hyemalis*), mergansers, and wood ducks (*Aix sponsa*), because the traditional survey area does not include a large portion of their breeding range. However, mergansers breed throughout a large portion of the eastern survey area. Therefore, the total-duck species composition in the eastern survey area includes these species. Estimates for canvasbacks, redheads, and ruddy ducks (*Oxyura jamaicensis*) are excluded from the eastern total-duck estimate because these species are rare breeders in this region. Wood ducks also are not included in the total-duck estimate for the eastern survey area, even though this species breeds over much of the region, as their wooded habitats make them difficult to detect from the air.

Mallard Fall-flight Index

The mallard fall-flight index is a prediction of the size of the fall abundance of mallards originating from the mid-continent region of North America. For management purposes, the mid-continent population is composed of mallards originating from the traditional survey area, as well as Michigan, Minnesota, and Wisconsin. The index is based on the mallard models used for Adaptive Harvest Management, and considers breeding population size, habitat conditions, adult summer survival, and projected fall age ratio (young/adult). The projected fall age ratio is predicted from a

model that depicts how the age ratio varies with changes in spring population size and pond abundance. The fall-flight index represents a weighted average of the fall flights predicted by the four alternative models of mallard population dynamics used in Adaptive Harvest Management (U. S. Fish and Wildlife Service 2005).

RESULTS AND DISCUSSION

2004 in Review

Most of the U.S. and Canadian prairies were much drier in May 2004 than in May 2003, which was reflected in the pond counts for these regions. For the U.S. Prairies and Canadian Prairie and Parkland combined, the May pond estimate was 3.9 ± 0.2 million, which was 24% lower than the 2003 estimate and 19% below the long-term average. Pond numbers in both Canada (2.5 ± 0.1 million) and the U. S. (1.4 ± 0.1 million) were below their 2003 estimates (-29% in Canada and -16% in the U.S). Canadian ponds were 25% below their long-term average.

The good water conditions that prevailed in 2003 on the short-grass prairies of southern Alberta and Saskatchewan did not continue into 2004, and habitat in these areas went from good to fair or poor. Habitat in southern Manitoba ranged from poor in the east-central to good in the west, with conditions similar to those of previous years. In the Dakotas, a slow drying trend continued, and much of eastern South Dakota was in poor condition. Conditions in the Dakotas were better to the north, and eastern Montana was a mosaic of poor to good conditions. Although prairie areas received considerable moisture from snow, including a late-spring snowstorm in southern regions, the snowmelt was absorbed by the parched ground. Furthermore, snow and cold during May probably adversely affected early nesters and young broods. Many prairie areas received abundant water after May surveys, but it likely did not alleviate dry conditions, because this precipitation also soaked into the ground. Therefore, overall expected production from the prairies was only poor to fair in 2004.

Spring thaw was exceptionally late in 2004 in the Northwest Territories, northern Alberta, northern Saskatchewan, and northern Manitoba. This meant that birds that over-flew the prairies due to poor conditions encountered winter-like conditions in the bush, and nesting may have been curtailed. This was especially true for early-nesting species like mallards and northern pintails; late nesters likely had better success. Overall, the bush regions were only fair to marginally good for production due to this late thaw. However, Alaska birds likely produced well due to excellent habitat conditions there. Areas south of the Brooks Range experienced a widespread, record-setting early spring breakup, and flooding of nesting areas was minimal.

Breeding habitat conditions in 2004 were generally good to excellent in the eastern U.S. and Canada. Although spring was late in most areas, it was thought nesting was not significantly affected because of abundant spring rain and mild temperatures during and following nesting. Production in the east was normal in Ontario and the Maritimes, and slightly below normal in Quebec.

In the traditional survey area, the total duck population estimate (excluding scoters, eiders, long-tailed ducks, mergansers, and wood ducks) was 32.2 ± 0.6 million birds, 11% below the 2003 estimate of 36.2 ± 0.7 million birds, and 3% below the long-term (1955-2003) average. In the eastern Dakotas, total duck numbers were similar to the previous year's estimate, and remained 29% above the long-term average. Counts in southern Alberta were also similar to last year's, and remained 42% below the long-term average. The total-duck estimate decreased 38% relative to 2003 in southern Saskatchewan and was 22% below the long-term average. Counts in central and northern Alberta, northeast British Columbia and the Northwest Territories were similar to the previous year's but below the long-term average. Counts in the northern Saskatchewan--northern Manitoba--western Ontario area, and the Alaska--Yukon Territory--Old Crow Flats region were both similar to 2003 estimates, but above their long-term averages. Total duck counts in the southern Manitoba region and the western Dakotas--eastern Montana region were similar to 2003 estimates and to long-term averages. The 2004 total duck population estimate for the eastern survey area was 3.9 ± 0.3 million birds. This estimate was similar to the previous year's (3.6 ± 0.3 million birds), and to the 1996-2003 average.

In British Columbia, California, northeastern U.S., Oregon, and Wisconsin, measures of precision for survey estimates are provided. In 2004, total duck abundance decreased by 23% in California relative to 2003, and was similar to 2003 estimates in British Columbia, Wisconsin, Oregon, and the northeastern U.S. The total duck estimate was down 31% in California and 16% in Oregon relative to the long-term average. In Wisconsin, total ducks were 58% above their long-term average. In British Columbia and the northeastern U.S., 2004 total duck estimates were similar to their long-term averages. Of the states without measures of precision for total duck numbers, estimates of total ducks increased in Nevada, Minnesota, and Michigan relative to 2003, but estimates decreased in Nebraska and Washington compared to the previous year.

Weather and habitat conditions during the summer months can influence waterfowl production. Good wetland conditions increase renesting effort and brood survival. In general, 2004 habitat conditions stabilized or improved over most of the traditional survey area between May and July. While there were no formal July surveys flown in 2004, experienced crew leaders in Montana and the western Dakotas, the eastern Dakotas, southern Alberta, and southern Saskatchewan returned to their May survey areas in early July to qualitatively assess habitat changes between May and July. Biologists from other survey areas communicated with local biologists to get their impressions of 2004 waterfowl production and monitored weather conditions. Habitat in some portions of the prairies, particularly in the Dakotas and Alberta, improved between May and July because of abundant summer rain. However, there were few birds in these areas because many had left the prairies in the early spring when habitat conditions were dry. Therefore, the production potential from most prairie areas ranged from poor to good and was generally worse than in 2003. Habitat conditions in the northern and eastern areas are more stable because of the deeper, more permanent water bodies there. Because temperatures were so cold in May of 2004, the outlook for production from these areas was fair in the northern Prairie Provinces, and good to excellent in the eastern survey area.

2005 Breeding Habitat Conditions, Populations, and Production

Overall Habitat and Population Status

Habitat conditions at the time of the survey in May 2005 were variable, with some areas improved relative to last year and others remaining or becoming increasingly dry. The total May pond estimate (Prairie and Parkland Canada and the northcentral U.S. combined) was 5.4 ± 0.2 million ponds. This was 37% greater than last year's estimate of 3.9 ± 0.2 million ponds and 12% higher than the long-term average of 4.8 ± 0.1 million ponds. Habitat in the surveyed portion of the U.S. prairies was in fair to poor condition due to a dry fall, winter, and early spring and warm

8

Table 1. Estimated number (in thousands) of May ponds in portions of prairie and parkland Canada and the northcentral U.S.

Survey Area	2005	2004	Change from 2004 %	Change from 2004 P	LTA[a]	Change from LTA %	Change from LTA P
Prairie Canada							
S. A berta	750	511	+47	0.007	721	+4	0.689
S. Saskatchewan	2415	1,461	+65	<0.001	1,953	+24	0.009
S. Manitoba	755	541	+40	0.001	671	+13	0.101
Subtotal	3,921	2,513	+56	<0.001	3,346	+17	0.004
Northcentral U.S.							
Montana and western Dakotas	663	597	+11	0.354	524	+27	0.016
Eastern Dakotas	798	810	-1	0.913	1,000	-20	<0.001
Subtotal	1,461	1,407	+4	0.678	1,524	-4	0.440
Grand Total	5,381	3,920	+37	<0.001	4,813	+12	0.008

[a]Long-term average. Prairie and parkland Canada, 1961-2004; northcentral U.S. and Grand Total, 1974-2004.

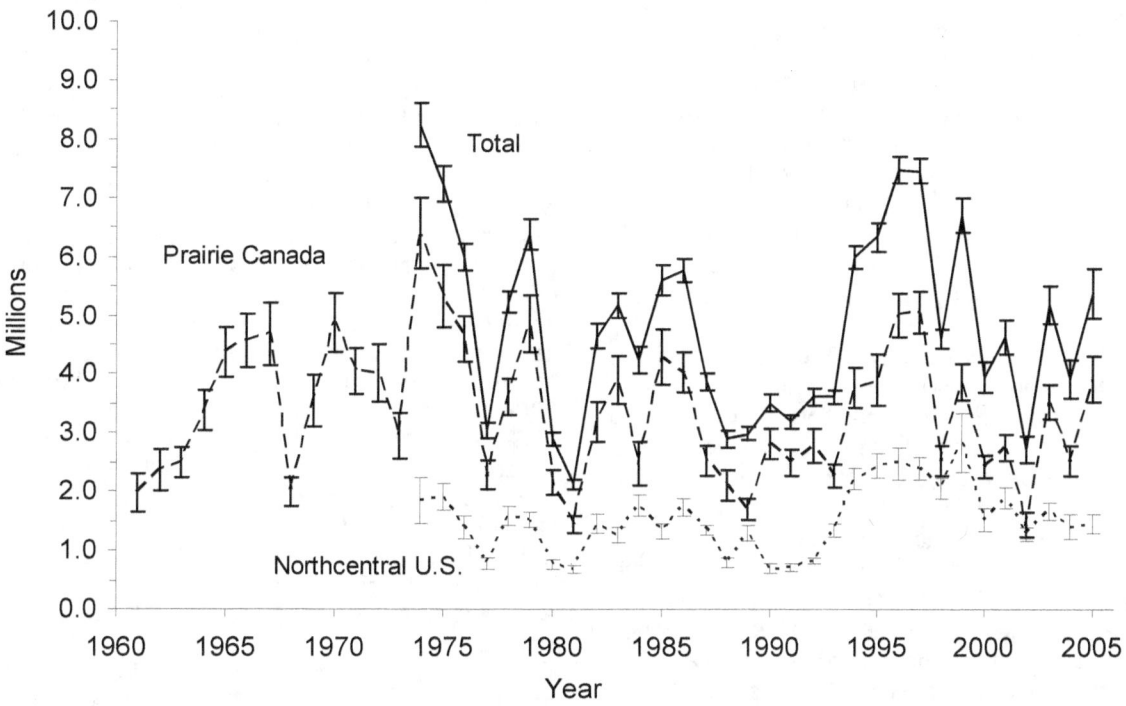

Figure 1. Number of ponds in May and 95% confidence intervals in prairie and parkland Canada and the northcentral U.S.

winter temperatures. Nesting habitat was particularly poor in South Dakota because of below average precipitation resulting in degraded wetland conditions and increased tilling and grazing of wetland margins. Birds may have over-flown the state for wetter conditions to the north. Water levels and upland nesting cover were relatively better in North Dakota and eastern Montana, and wetland conditions in these regions improved markedly during June following the survey, with the onset of well-above average precipitation.

The 2005 pond estimate for north-central U.S. (1.5 ± 0.1 million) was similar to last year's estimate (Fig. 2). The prairies of southern Alberta and southwestern Saskatchewan were also quite dry in early May. The U.S. and Canadian prairies received substantial rain in late May and during the entire month of June that recharged wetlands and encouraged growth of vegetation. While this improved habitat quality on the Prairies, it probably came too late to benefit early-nesting species or prevent overflight. This heavy rain likely benefited late-nesting species and improved renesting. Record high rains flooded the lower elevation prairie areas of central Manitoba during April, producing fair or poor nesting conditions for breeding waterfowl. In contrast, the Canadian Parklands were much improved compared to last year, due to several years of improving nesting cover and above-normal precipitation last fall and winter. These areas were in good-to-excellent condition at the start of the survey and remained so into July. Overall, the May pond estimate in Prairie and Parkland Canada was 3.9 ± 0.2 million. This was a 56% increase over last year's estimate of 2.5 ± 0.1 million ponds and 17% higher than the long-term average of 3.3 ± 0.3 million ponds.

Portions of northern Manitoba and northern Saskatchewan also experienced flooding, resulting in only fair conditions for breeding waterfowl. In contrast, most of the Northwest Territories was in good condition due to adequate water and a timely spring break-up that made habitat available to early-nesting species. However, dry conditions in eastern parts of the Northwest Territories and northern Alberta resulted in low water levels in lakes and ponds and the complete drying of some wetlands. Therefore, habitat was also classified as fair in these areas. For the most part, habitats in Alaska were in excellent condition, with an early spring and good water levels, except for a few flooded

river areas and on the North Slope, where spring was late.

In the Eastern Survey Area (strata 51-72), habitat conditions were generally good due to adequate water and relatively mild spring temperatures. Exceptions were the coast of Maine and the Atlantic Provinces, where May temperatures were cool and some flooding occurred along the coast and major rivers. Also, below-normal precipitation left some habitat in fair to poor condition in southern Ontario. However, precipitation in southern Ontario after survey completion improved habitat conditions in that region.

In the traditional survey area, the total duck population estimate (excluding scoters, eiders, long-tailed ducks, mergansers, and wood ducks) was 31.7 ± 0.6 million birds, similar to last year's estimate of 32.2 ± 0.6 million birds, and 5% below the long-term (1955-2004) average (Table 2, Appendix G). In the eastern Dakotas, total duck numbers were 14% below last year's estimate, but remained 10% above the long-term average. Counts in southern Alberta were 27% higher than those last year, but remained 26% below the long-term average. The total-duck estimate increased 38% relative to last year in southern Saskatchewan and was 9% above the long-term average. Total duck estimates in central and northern Alberta, northeastern British Columbia and the Northwest Territories were 20% below last year's estimate and 35% below the long-term average (Table 2). Counts in the western Ontario--northern Saskatchewan--northern Manitoba area, and the western Dakotas--Eastern Montana area were 21% and 20% below 2004 estimates, respectively, and 10% and 20% below their long-term averages. In the Alaska--Yukon Territory--Old Crow Flats region the total duck estimate was similar to that of 2004, but remained 45% above its long-term average. Total duck counts in southern Manitoba remained unchanged from the 2004 estimate and the long-term average

Several states and provinces conduct breeding waterfowl surveys in areas outside the geographic extent of the Waterfowl Breeding Population and Habitat Survey of the USFWS and CWS. In British Columbia, California, northeastern U.S., Oregon, and Wisconsin, measures of precision for survey estimates are available. Total duck abundance increased by 49% in California relative to 2004, and was similar to 2004 in British Columbia, Wisconsin, and the northeastern U.S. The total duck estimate was similar to the long-term average in California. In Wisconsin, total ducks were 73% above their long-

Table 2. Total duck[a] breeding population estimates (in thousands).

Region	2005	2004	Change from 2004		LTA[b]	Change from LTA	
			%	P		%	P
Traditional Survey Area							
Alaska - Yukon Territory - Old Crow Flats	5,114	5,456	-6	0.194	3,519	+45	<0.001
C. & N. Alberta - N.E. British Columbia - Northwest Territories	4,713	5,882	-20	0.001	7,202	-35	<0.001
N. Saskatchewan - N. Manitoba - W. Ontario	3,223	4,085	-21	0.007	3,564	-10	0.099
S. Alberta	3,178	2,499	+27	0.002	4,305	-26	<0.001
S. Saskatchewan	7,967	5,783	+38	<0.001	7,336	+9	0.024
S. Manitoba	1,627	1,474	+10	0.172	1,542	+5	0.287
Montana and Western Dakotas	1,290	1,615	-20	0.006	1,620	-20	<0.001
Eastern Dakotas	4,623	5,370	-14	0.022	4,193	+10	0.067
Total	31,735	32,164	-1	0.593	33,281	-5	0.006
Other Regions							
British Columbia[c]	6	7	-15	0.530	6	-14	0.458
California	615	413	+49	0.010	599	+3	0.820
Northeastern U.S.[d]	1,416	1,417	-1	0.997	143	-1	0.907
Oregon	225	245	-8	0.377	302	-25	<0.001
Wisconsin	724	651	+11	0.462	420	+73	<0.001

[a] Excludes eider, long-tailed duck, wood duck, scoter, and merganser in traditional survey area; excludes eider, long-tailed duck, wood duck, redhead, canvasback and ruddy duck in eastern survey area; species composition for other regions varies.
[b] Long-term average. Traditional survey area=1955-2004; years for other regions vary (see Appendix E).
[c] Index to waterfowl use in prime waterfowl producing regions of the province. Estimates do not match those from previous reports because of change in analytical method.
[d] Includes all or portions of CT, DE, MD, MA, NH, NJ, NY, PA, RI, VT, and VA.
[e] Not estimable from current survey.

Table 3. Mallard breeding population estimates (in thousands).

Region	2005	2004	Change from 2004 %	Change from 2004 P	LTA[b]	Change from LTA %	Change from LTA P
Traditional Survey Area							
Alaska - Yukon Territory - Old Crow Flats	703	811	-13	0.199	350	+101	<0.001
C. & N. Alberta - N.E. British Columbia - Northwest Territories	533	776	-31	0.025	1,097	-51	<0.001
N. Saskatchewan - N. Manitoba - W. Ontario	937	1,283	-27	0.143	1,163	-19	0.165
S. Alberta	671	600	+12	0.460	1,107	-39	<0.001
S. Saskatchewan	1,729	1,609	+7	0.515	2,079	-17	0.007
S. Manitoba	455	393	+16	0.194	377	+21	0.054
Montana and Western Dakotas	387	495	-22	0.160	502	-23	0.017
Eastern Dakotas	1,340	1,456	-8	0.520	836	+60	<0.001
Total	6,755	7,425	-9	0.092	7,510	-10	0.008
Eastern Survey Area							
Other Regions							
British Columbia[b]	1	1	-16	0.436	1	-22	0.064
California	318	262	+21	0.341	372	-15	0.275
Michigan	230	329	-30	0.075	428	-46	<0.001
Minnesota	239	375	-36	0.033	223	+7	d
Northeastern U.S.[c]	754	806	-6	0.483	804	-6	0.367
Oregon	83	92	-10	0.342	113	-26	<0.001
Wisconsin	317	229	+38	0.087	175	+81	0.001

[a] Long-term average. Traditional survey area=1955-2004; eastern survey area=1999-2004; years for other regions vary (see Appendix E).
[b] Index to waterfowl use in prime waterfowl producing regions of the province. Estimates do not match those from previous reports because of change in analytical method.
[c] Includes all or portions of CT, DE, MD, MA, NH, NJ, NY, PA, RI, VT, and VA.
[d] Value for test statistic was not available.

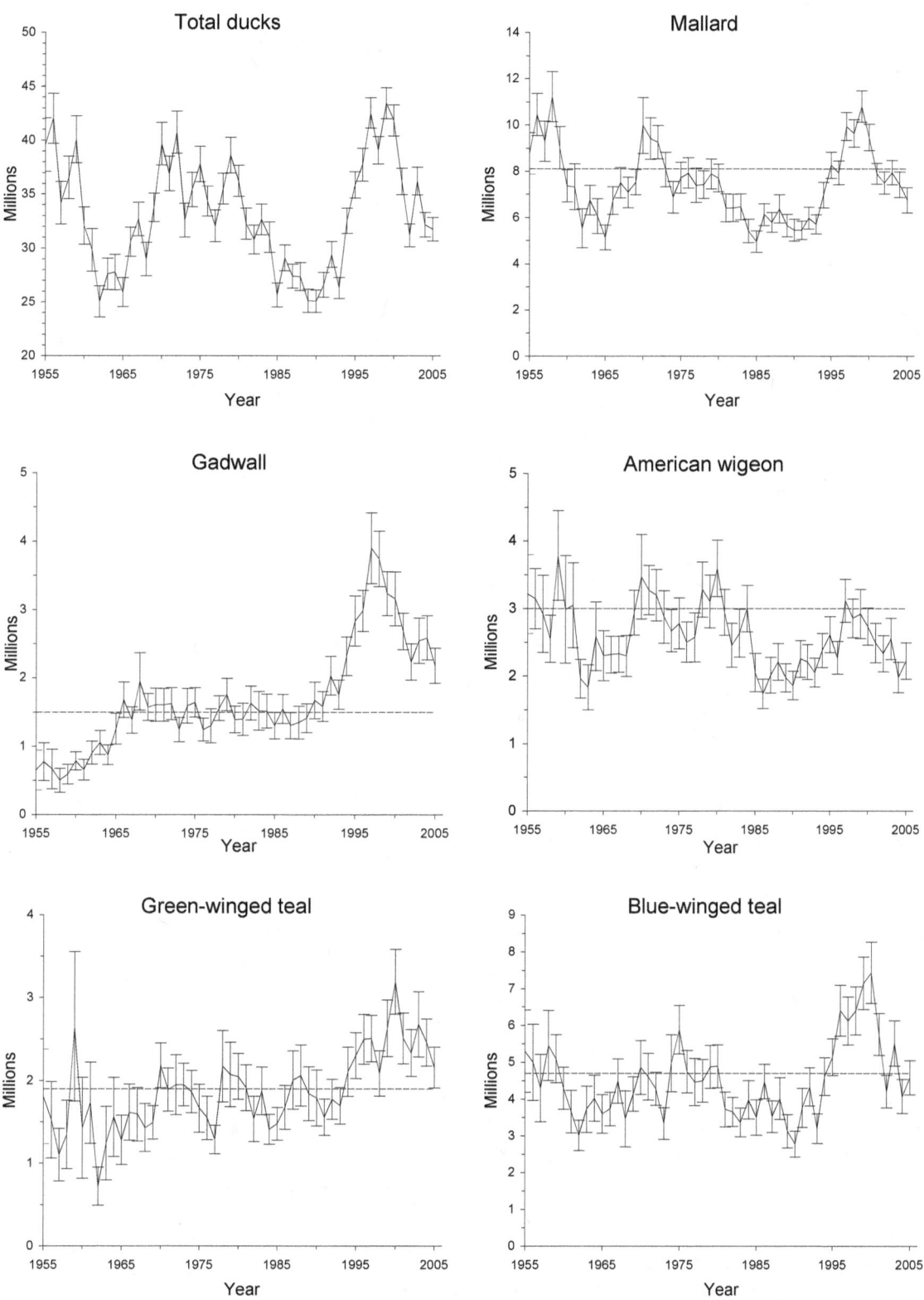

Figure 2. Breeding population estimates, 95% confidence intervals, and North American Waterfowl Management Plan population goal (dashed line) for selected species in the traditional survey area (strata 1-18, 20-50, 75-77).

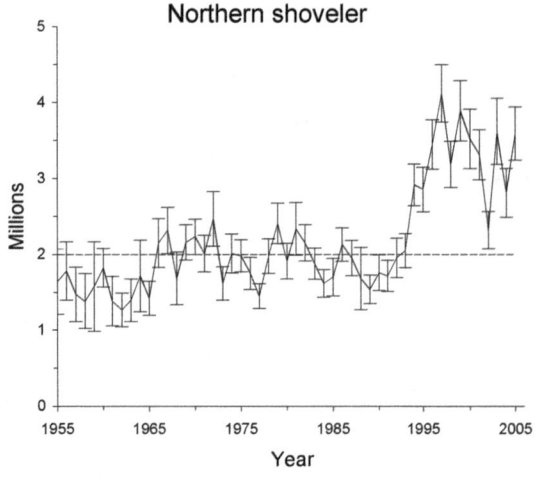

Northern shoveler

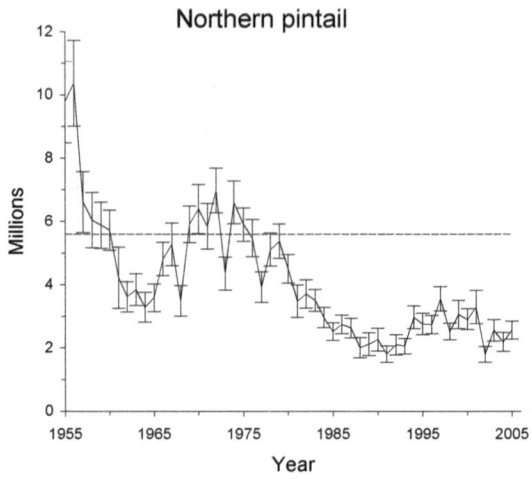

Northern pintail

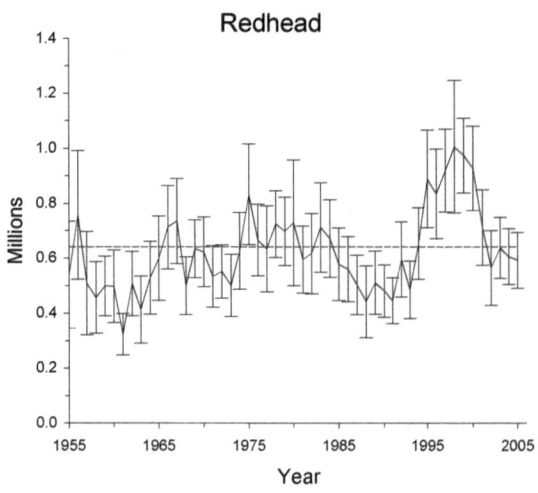

Redhead

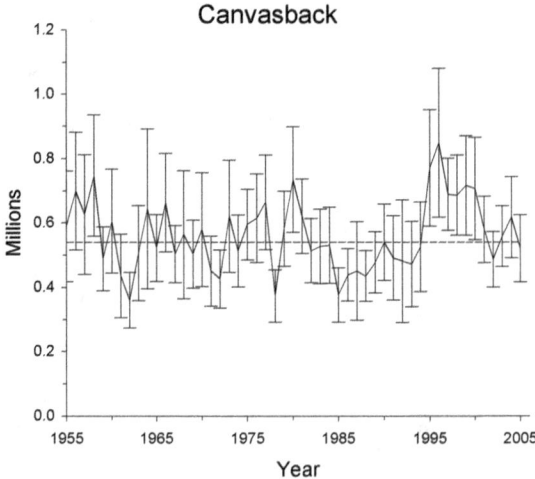

Canvasback

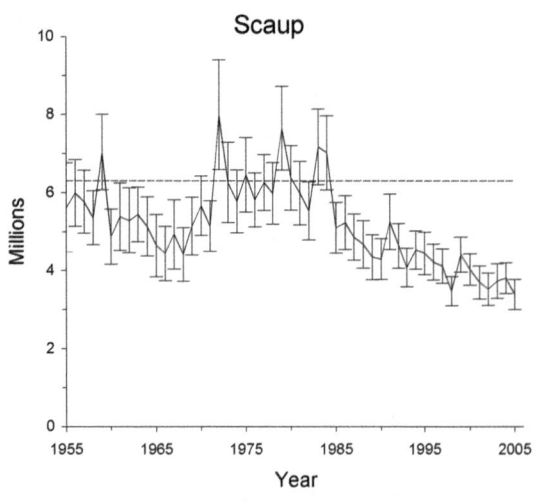

Scaup

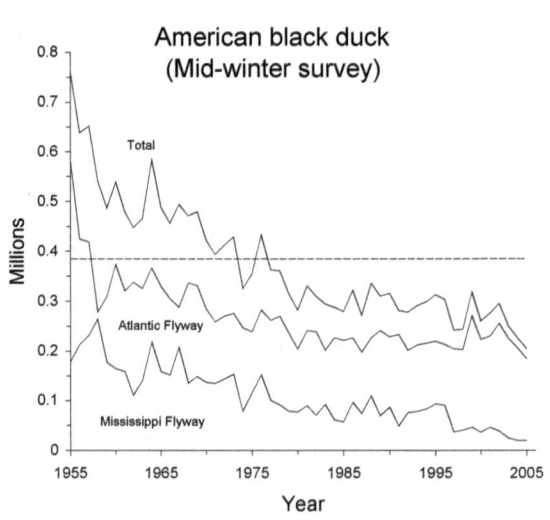

American black duck
(Mid-winter survey)

Figure 2 (continued).

term average. In British Columbia, California, and the northeastern U.S., total duck estimates were similar to their long-term averages. Of the states without measures of precision for total duck numbers, estimates of total ducks decreased in Nevada, Minnesota, Washington, Oregon, and Michigan, and increased in Nevada, relative to 2004.

Trends and annual breeding population estimates for 10 principal duck species from the traditional survey area are provided in Figure 2, Tables 3-12, and Appendix F. Mallard abundance was 6.8 ± 0.3 million, which was 9% lower than last year's estimate of 7.4 ± 0.3 million, and 10% lower than the long-term average (Table 3). Mallard numbers dropped 31% relative to last year's estimate in the central and northern Alberta--northeastern British Columbia--Northwest Territories survey area, but remained unchanged relative to 2004 in all other survey areas. Mallard numbers remained 101% above their long-term average in the Alaska--Yukon Territory--Old Crow Flats region, and were 60% and 21% higher than the long-term averages in the eastern Dakotas and southern Manitoba, respectively. Mallards were 17% below their long-term average in southern Saskatchewan, and 23% below in Montana and the western Dakotas. Mallard estimates for the central and northern Alberta--- northeastern British Columbia--Northwest Territories were also below their long-term average (-51%). In the northern Saskatchewan-- northern Manitoba--western Ontario survey area the mallard estimate was similar to its long-term average. In other areas where surveys are conducted and measures of precision for estimates are provided (the same states as for total ducks, as well as Michigan and Minnesota), mallard abundance remained unchanged from 2004, except for Michigan (-30%) and Wisconsin (+38%). Mallard estimates were below the long-term average in Michigan, British Columbia, and Oregon, similar to the long-term average in California, and the northeastern U. S., and above it in Wisconsin. In Nebraska, Nevada and Washington, estimates of precision are unavailable, but mallard counts were down relative to last year's in Nevada, higher than last year's counts in Nebraska, and were similar in Washington.

Blue-winged teal abundance was estimated at 4.6 ± 0.2 million birds, 13% higher than last year's estimate of 4.1 ± 0.2 million birds and similar to the 1955-2004 average. Of the other duck species, gadwall (2.2 ± 0.1 million) dropped 16% relative to 2004 but remained 30% above their long-term average. American wigeon (2.2 ± 0.1 million) and scaup (3.4 ± 0.2 million) were similar to their 2004 estimates, but were 15% and 35%

below their long-term averages, respectively. Green-winged teal (2.2 ± 0.1 million) were also similar to their 2004 estimate, but were 16% higher than their long-term average. Northern pintails (2.6 ± 0.2 million) increased by 17% relative to last year, but remained 38% below their long-term average. The northern shoveler estimate was 28% higher than last year's, and 67% higher than the long-term average. Redhead (0.6 ± 0.1 million), and canvasback (0.5 ± 0.1 million) estimates were similar to their 2004 estimates and long-term averages.

Populations of all the six species in the eastern survey area that we reported were similar to their 1999-2004 estimates (Table 13, Appendix H). Mergansers, mallards, American black ducks, and green-winged teal were 25%, 36%, 24% and 46% below their 2004 estimates. The ring-necked duck and goldeneye estimates were similar to those of 2004.

The longest time-series of data available to assess the status of the American black duck (*Anas rubripes*) is provided by the Midwinter surveys conducted in January in states of the Atlantic and Mississippi Flyways. The trend in the winter index for the total population is depicted in Figure 2. Measures of precision are not available for the midwinter surveys. Midwinter counts of American black ducks (203,900 in both flyways combined) declined relative to 2004 counts. This was 10% lower than the 2004 index of 226,700, and 25% lower than the 10-year mean (272,600). In the Atlantic Flyway, the midwinter index of 184,100 decreased 11% from 206,400 in 2004, and was 18% below the most recent 10-year mean (225,000). In the Mississippi Flyway, the American black duck mid-winter index decreased 2% from 20,300 in 2004 to 19,900, which is 58% below the 10-year mean (47,600). A shorter time series for assessing change in American black duck population status is provided by the breeding waterfowl surveys conducted by the USFWS and CWS in the eastern survey area. In the eastern survey area, the 2004 estimate for breeding American black ducks (827,000) was down 24% compared to last year's estimate (1,093,000) but similar to the 1999-2004 average (1,002,000).

Trends in wood duck populations are monitored by the North American Breeding Bird Survey (BBS), a series of roadside routes surveyed during May and June each year. Wood ducks are encountered with low frequency along BBS routes, limiting the amount and quality of available information for analysis (Sauer and Droege 1990). However, the BBS provides the only long-term indices of this species' regional populations. Trend analysis suggests that wood duck numbers increased 3.8% per year over

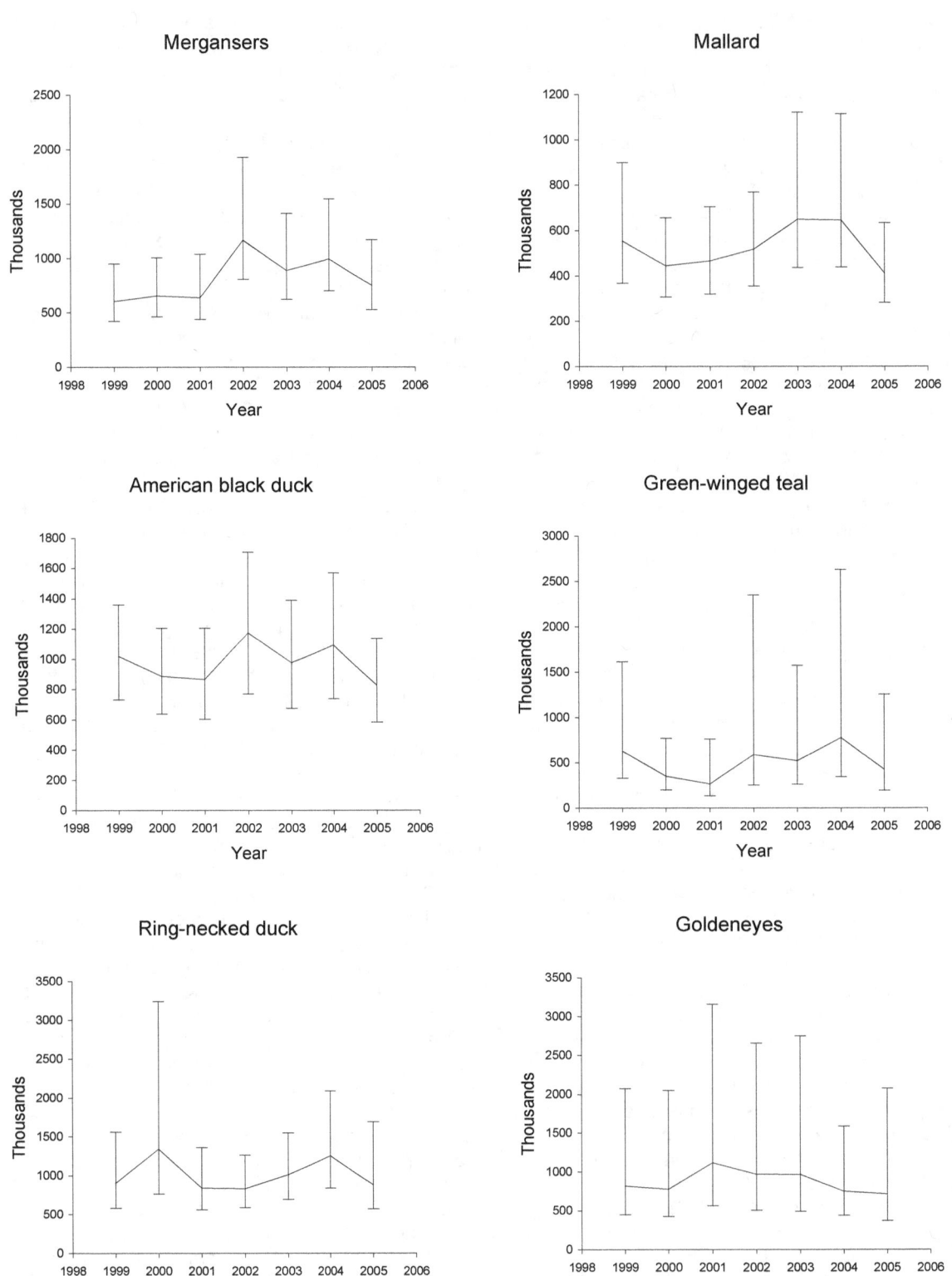

Figure 3. Median population size and credibility intervals for 6 species in the Eastern survey area (strata 51-72).

Table 4. Gadwall breeding population estimates (in thousands) for regions in the traditional survey area.

Region	2005	2004	Change from 2004		LTA	Change from LTA	
			%	P		%	P
Alaska-Yukon Territory – Old Crow Flats	3	2	+42	0.734	2	+43	0.705
C. & N. Alberta – N.E. British Columbia - Northwest Territories	77	138	-44	0.083	46	+66	0.050
N. Saskatchewan- N. Manitoba - W. Ontario	19	22	-16	0.772	28	-32	0.133
S. Alberta	338	290	+17	0.492	308	+10	0.612
S. Saskatchewan	723	752	-4	0.847	553	+31	0.052
S. Manitoba	120	148	-18	0.362	65	+84	<0.001
Montana and western Dakotas	187	205	-9	0.614	194	-4	0.797
Eastern Dakotas	712	1,033	-31	0.006	486	+46	0.001
Total	2,179	2,590	-16	0.052	1,683	+30	<0.001

Table 5. American wigeon breeding population estimates (in thousands) for regions in the traditional survey area.

Region	2005	2004	Change from 2004		LTA	Change from LTA	
			%	P		%	P
Alaska-Yukon Territory – Old Crow Flats	873	897	-3	0.790	504	+73	<0.001
C. & N. Alberta – N.E. British Columbia - Northwest Territories	583	565	+3	0.889	919	-36	0.002
N. Saskatchewan- N. Manitoba - W. Ontario	174	149	+17	0.568	254	-31	0.013
S. Alberta	125	117	+8	0.728	300	-58	<0.001
S. Saskatchewan	294	128	+130	0.002	428	-31	0.006
S. Manitoba	34	3	+893	0.002	62	-45	0.006
Montana and western Dakotas	67	66	+2	0.926	110	-39	<0.001
Eastern Dakotas	73	56	+30	0.405	48	+53	0.114
Total	2,225	1,981	+12	0.177	2,624	-15	0.005

Table 6. Green-winged teal breeding population estimates (in thousands) for regions in the traditional survey area.

Region	2005	2004	Change from 2004		LTA	Change from LTA	
			%	P		%	P
Alaska-Yukon Territory – Old Crow Flats	713	819	-13	0.289	351	+103	<0.001
C. & N. Alberta – N.E. British Columbia - Northwest Territories	437	835	-48	0.002	759	-42	<0.001
N. Saskatchewan- N. Manitoba - W. Ontario	310	375	-17	0.262	195	+59	0.002
S. Alberta	159	98	+61	0.138	195	-18	0.291
S. Saskatchewan	359	124	+189	<0.001	227	+58	0.027
S. Manitoba	55	27	+103	0.007	52	+7	0.686
Montana and western Dakotas	83	104	-20	0.395	39	+113	0.008
Eastern Dakotas	42	79	-47	0.079	45	-8	0.742
Total	2,157	2,461	-12	0.114	1,861	+16	0.021

Table 7. Blue-winged teal breeding population estimates (in thousands) for regions in the traditional survey area.

Region	2005	2004	Change from 2004		LTA	Change from LTA	
			%	P		%	P
Alaska-Yukon Territory – Old Crow Flats	3	2	+25	0.876	1	+105	0.626
C. & N. Alberta – N.E. British Columbia - Northwest Territories	247	401	-38	0.116	271	-9	0.704
N. Saskatchewan- N. Manitoba - W. Ontario	139	60	+130	0.102	268	-48	0.007
S. Alberta	649	360	+80	0.009	608	+7	0.665
S. Saskatchewan	1,597	1,155	+38	0.026	1,210	+32	0.002
S. Manitoba	339	282	+20	0.206	383	-12	0.207
Montana and western Dakotas	286	320	-10	0.508	263	+9	0.467
Eastern Dakotas	1,325	1,493	-11	0.427	1,496	-11	0.275
Total	4,586	4,073	+13	0.126	4,499	+2	0.720

Table 8. Northern shoveler breeding population estimates (in thousands) for regions in the traditional survey area.

| Region | 2005 | 2004 | Change from 2004 | | LTA | Change from LTA | |
			%	P		%	P
Alaska-Yukon Territory – Old Crow Flats	666	643	+4	0.806	259	+158	<0.001
C. & N. Alberta – N.E. British Columbia - Northwest Territories	213	247	-14	0.554	213	0	0.992
N. Saskatchewan- N. Manitoba - W. Ontario	29	33	-13	0.683	43	-34	0.016
S. Alberta	548	385	+42	0.133	356	+54	0.018
S. Saskatchewan	1,314	784	+68	0.001	634	+107	<0.001
S. Manitoba	211	143	+47	0.176	105	+100	0.004
Montana and western Dakotas	148	200	-26	0.204	149	-1	0.959
Eastern Dakotas	464	377	+23	0.212	388	+19	0.170
Total	3,591	2,810	+28	0.001	2,149	+67	<0.001

Table 9. Northern pintail breeding population estimates (in thousands) for regions in the traditional survey area.

| Region | 2005 | 2004 | Change from 2004 | | LTA | Change from LTA | |
			%	P		%	P
Alaska-Yukon Territory – Old Crow Flats	905	927	-2	0.856	913	-1	0.939
C. & N. Alberta – N.E. British Columbia - Northwest Territories	108	193	-44	0.073	384	-72	<0.001
N. Saskatchewan- N. Manitoba - W. Ontario	8	10	-18	0.672	42	-80	<0.001
S. Alberta	282	161	+75	0.049	730	-61	<0.001
S. Saskatchewan	858	474	+81	0.009	1,225	-30	<0.001
S. Manitoba	68	40	+71	0.042	113	-40	<0.001
Montana and western Dakotas	75	132	-43	0.031	273	-73	<0.001
Eastern Dakotas	256	247	+4	0.860	463	-45	<0.001
Total	2,561	2,185	+17	0.079	4,142	-38	<0.001

Table 10. Redhead breeding population estimates (in thousands) for regions in the traditional survey area.

| Region | 2005 | 2004 | Change from 2004 | | LTA | Change from LTA | |
			%	P		%	P
Alaska-Yukon Territory – Old Crow Flats	<1	2	-91	0.044	1	-84	<0.001
C. & N. Alberta – N.E. British Columbia - Northwest Territories	49	73	-33	0.304	38	+30	0.530
N. Saskatchewan- N. Manitoba - W. Ontario	13	31	-57	0.136	28	-53	<0.001
S. Alberta	91	79	+16	0.648	117	-22	0.170
S. Saskatchewan	226	131	+72	0.02	189	+19	0.251
S. Manitoba	98	102	-4	0.900	71	+37	0.338
Montana and western Dakotas	3	25	-89	0.102	10	-70	0.002
Eastern Dakotas	112	161	-31	0.102	170	-34	0.002
Total	592	605	-2	0.858	625	-5	0.536

Table 11. Canvasback breeding population estimates (in thousands) for regions in the traditional survey area.

| Region | 2005 | 2004 | Change from 2004 | | LTA | Change from LTA | |
			%	P		%	P
Alaska-Yukon Territory – Old Crow Flats	95	161	-41	0.207	91	+4	0.887
C. & N. Alberta – N.E. British Columbia - Northwest Territories	98	109	-11	0.768	72	+35	0.416
N. Saskatchewan- N. Manitoba - W. Ontario	39	50	-21	0.578	56	-30	0.253
S. Alberta	43	50	-15	0.758	64	-33	0.104
S. Saskatchewan	162	121	+34	0.181	183	-11	0.425
S. Manitoba	48	70	-32	0.344	56	-15	0.518
Montana and western Dakotas	5	12	-60	0.046	8	-39	0.095
Eastern Dakotas	31	44	-28	0.275	33	-5	0.817
Total	521	617	-16	0.247	563	-8	0.433

Table 12. Scaup (greater and lesser combined) breeding population estimates (in thousands) for regions in the traditional survey area.

| Region | 2005 | 2004 | Change from 2004 | | LTA | Change from LTA | |
			%	P		%	P
Alaska-Yukon Territory – Old Crow Flats	961	982	-2	0.865	914	+5	0.593
C. & N. Alberta – N.E. British Columbia - Northwest Territories	1,361	1,624	-16	0.232	2,653	-49	<0.001
N. Saskatchewan- N. Manitoba - W. Ontario	349	582	-40	<0.001	592	-41	<0.001
S. Alberta	127	124	+2	0.948	358	-65	<0.001
S. Saskatchewan	381	185	+106	0.008	417	-9	0.595
S. Manitoba	60	31	+91	0.019	137	-56	<0.001
Montana and western Dakotas	16	28	-41	0.309	54	-70	<0.001
Eastern Dakotas	132	251	-47	0.034	96	+37	0.162
Total	3,387	3,807	-11	0.136	5,220	-35	<0.001

Table 13. Duck breeding population estimates (median, in thousands) for 6 species in the eastern survey area.

Species	2005	2004	% Change from 2004	Average [a]	% Change from average
Mergansers (common, red-breasted, & hooded)	753	995	-25 [b]	825	-9
Mallard	412	646	-36 [b]	546	-25
American black duck	827	1093	-24 [b]	1002	-18
American green-winged teal	121	226	-46 [b]	150	-20
Ring-necked duck	883	1257	-30	1032	-14
Goldeneye (common & Barrow's)	715	748	-5	901	-21

[a] Average for 1999-2004.

[b] Significant ($P<0 05$) determined by non-overlap of Bayesian credibility intervals.

the long-term (1966-2004) and 1.9% over the short-term (1985-2004), in the Atlantic and Mississippi Flyways combined. Specifically, in the Atlantic Flyway, the BBS indicated a 4.8% annual increase in wood ducks over the long-term, and a 2.4% annual increase over the intermediate-term (1985-2004). In the Mississippi Flyway, the BBS indicated a 3.3% annual increase over the long-term, and a 1.7% annual increase over the intermediate-term. Analysis of short-term wood duck BBS data over the past 10-year period (1995-2004) yielded no significant trend for the Atlantic or Mississippi Flyways, or the two flyways combined (J. Sauer, U. S. Geological Survey/Biological Resources Division, unpublished data).

Weather and habitat conditions during the summer months can influence waterfowl production. Good wetland conditions generally increase renesting effort and brood survival. In general, 2005 habitat conditions improved over most of the traditional survey area between May and July. While no formal July surveys were flown this year, experienced crew leaders in Montana and the western Dakotas, the eastern Dakotas, southern Alberta, and southern Saskatchewan returned to their May survey areas in early July to qualitatively assess habitat changes between May and July. Biologists from other survey areas communicated with local biologists to get their impressions of 2005 waterfowl production and monitored weather conditions. Habitat on most of the prairies, especially southern Saskatchewan and eastern Montana improved between May and July because of abundant summer rain. Even in Alberta, where a severe drought prevailed in May, conditions have dramatically improved. For birds that did not overfly the praries, prospects for production are good. Habitat conditions in the northern and eastern areas tend to be more stable because of the deeper, more permanent water bodies there. In general, the outlook for production was rated fair to good in the northern Prairie Provinces and good to excellent in the eastern survey area.

Regional Habitat and Population Status

A description of habitat conditions, populations, and production for each for the major breeding areas follows. More detailed reports of specific regions are available in *Waterfowl Population Surveys* reports, located on the Division of Migratory Bird Management's home page. Some of the habitat information that follows was taken from these reports (http://migratorybirds.fws.gov/reports/reports.html).

Southern Alberta: During the fall and winter of 2004/2005 most of prairie southern Alberta (strata 27, 28 and 29) received only 20-60% of normal precipitation, except in western areas near Rocky Mountain House, High River and Claresholm, where much higher-than-normal precipitation occurred. Spring runoff was below average in prairie Alberta. Precipitation during April generally ranged from 25 to 50% of normal in western areas of Alberta from Grande Prairie south to Pincher Creek. Southeastern Alberta also had below-normal April precipitation. Overall, habitat conditions were poor when the survey was flown.

However, the Aspen Parkland areas of strata 26 and 75 were improved compared to the past few years. Greater-than-normal precipitation was recorded in the fall and spring in a band across the province from Peace River (145% of normal) to Cold Lake (98% of normal) and south to Lloydminster (114% of normal). Habitat conditions ranged from fair in southern stratum 26 to good in the northern areas of strata 26 and 75. Winter precipitation in the Grande Prairie area was near normal. Habitat in the Peace Parklands of northcentral Alberta improved from generally poor last year to fair-good.

Overall, May ponds were up 47% relative to 2004, and were similar to the long-term average. In response, total duck (+27%) and northern pintail (+75%) numbers were considerably higher than in 2004, but remained 26% and 61% below their long-term averages,. Mallards (-39%), American wigeon (-58%), and scaup (-65%) were all below their long-term averages, but similar to last year's estimates. The northern shoveler estimate was similar to last year's, but they are the only species in this survey area with counts above (+54%) their long-term average. Blue-winged teal numbers were 80% higher than in 2004, but similar to their long-term average. Gadwall, green-winged teal, redhead and canvasback estimates were all similar to their 2004 counts and long-term averages.

As of July 2005, the western prairies of Alberta had improved considerably. Eastern portions of the prairies are still in poor condition. This area has suffered under a drought for several years and will require quite a bit of above-normal precipitation for wetland and upland habitat to recover. The Aspen Parklands of strata 26 were very wet due to the above-normal June rains. Most areas were in good to fair condition in July, an improvement over May. In strata 75-76, Palmer drought indices suggested habitat had improved since May. There was little evidence of renesting, perhaps due to June flooding in some areas, or because those rains came too late to stimulate a good renesting effort. Most of the water received in June absorbed into the dry soil in strata 27, 28, and 29. However, in stratum 26 wetlands were recharged and duckling production appeared improved relative to last year and 2003.

Southern Saskatchewan: The grasslands of strata 32 and 33 received average to below-average precipitation during the winter. Spring precipitation was patchy across the grasslands during April and May and much of the area continued to receive only average precipitation; the exceptions were in the southwest and northwest, which received above average rainfall. Upland habitat throughout the grasslands appeared to be in better shape than in 2004. As of May, predicted production from the grasslands ranged from poor in the western and southern grasslands to fair in the southwest and central survey areas, and good along the Missouri Coteau into the Alan Hills and west to the Alberta border.

The extreme northwestern grasslands had excellent water and habitat conditions, and ducks were present in high numbers. The northwestern parklands (stratum 30) received above-average precipitation during the winter and spring and both upland nesting cover and wetlands were in good to excellent condition. The northeastern parklands received below-average to average precipitation during the winter and average to above-average precipitation during the spring. Most of the upland and wetland habitat within the stratum was in good to excellent condition for duck nesting and brood rearing.

The May pond estimate was 65% higher than last year's count, and was 24% above the long-term average. Total ducks were 38% above their 2004 counts, and 9% higher than their long-term average. Except for mallards, gadwall and canvasbacks, which were unchanged from their 2004 estimates, all other species in the region were higher than their 2004 estimates. American wigeon (+130%), green-winged teal (+189%), blue-winged teal (+38%), northern shovelers (+68%), northern pintails (+81%) and redheads (+72%) were all vastly improved relative to their 2004 estimates. However, northern pintails, American wigeon, and mallards remained 30%, 31%, and 17% below their long-term averages, respectively. Redheads were similar to their long-term average. Green-winged teal (+58%), gadwall +31%), blue-winged teal (+32%), and northern

shoveler (+107%) numbers were well above long-term averages. Scaup were 106% above their 2004 estimate, but similar to their long-term average. Canvasbacks were similar to their 2004 estimate and long-term average.

The northeast parklands region (stratum 31) remained in excellent condition during the weeks following the May survey. Upland habitat was in good condition and most of this area had good-excellent wetland conditions, with some flooded crops. The northwest portion of the parklands also had good-excellent habitat in July. Sheetwater was evident in many portions of stratum 32, north and east of Kindersley, and southeast of Regina. Stratum 33 was rated fair-good, and conditions had improved since May. Stratum 30 was drier than in May, but still had good brood water and excellent cover. Southeastern Saskatchewan (Strata 34 and 35) also received much water and had excellent wetland conditions. However, many wetlands were void of ducks, and production may have been hampered due to flooding. Overall, the survey area was rated good-excellent for re-nesting potential and duckling production.

Southern Manitoba: Habitat conditions for breeding waterfowl have improved over last year in southern Manitoba (strata 24, 36-40). Above-average precipitation in the fall and winter and rapid snowmelt in March resulted in heavy runoff into wetland basins this spring. The southwestern part of this survey region (strata 39 and 40) was in excellent condition, and as of May, along with southeastern Saskatchewan, was the only large portion of the Prairies so classified. The rest of the survey area (stratum 25) also had improved water conditions, but more wet weather was needed to improve residual cover, which is still sparse. As of May, good production was expected from this area, provided weather conditions remained favorable for the rest of the spring and summer.

The May pond count was 40% higher than the 2004 estimate, but similar to the long-term average. Total ducks, blue-winged teal, redheads, and canvasbacks were similar to their 2004 estimates and long-term averages. Mallards were similar to their 2004 estimate, but 21% above their long-term average. Northern pintail (+71%) and scaup (+91%) estimates were higher than to those of 2004, but remained 40% and 56% below their long-term averages, respectively. The gadwall estimate was unchanged relative to last year, and was 84% above the long-term average. The American wigeon estimate improved dramatically (+893%) relative to last year's record low, but remained 45% below the long term average for the survey area. Green-winged teal numbers were also higher than last year (+103%) but similar to their long-term average. Northern shoveler numbers were similar to last year's, but were 100% above their long-term average.

Manitoba received much higher than normal precipitation from May to July, which made for excellent brood-rearing habitat, but flooding may have destroyed waterfowl nests in many areas. As of July, the southwestern corner of Manitoba remained in excellent condition. A band of habitat running from Minnedosa south through Brandon was rated good for production. Conditions worsened to the east, with stratum 25, and the areas just to the west of Lake Manitoba and Lake Winnipegosis rated only fair. The center of the province along the North Dakota border was also rated good. In strata 37 and 38, east of Lake Manitoba, conditions were poor for duck production. Overall however, good to excellent production was expected in southern Manitoba.

Montana and Western Dakotas: In May, conditions in the Western Dakotas and Montana (Strata 41-44) were much drier this year than they were the same time last year, due to lack of precipitation in the fall and winter coupled with warm winter temperatures. Overall, conditions for breeding waterfowl were rated fair to poor.

The region roughly north of the Missouri River in eastern Montana (stratum 41) experienced a mild winter following a relatively dry fall in 2004. By early May precipitation was less than 50% of normal with less than average amounts of run off along the western portion of the region. The border between U.S. and Saskatchewan/Alberta, an important northern pintail area, was only fair. Conditions were poor in the region between Havre and Great Falls, but improved between Glasgow and Plentywood. During the latter part of the 2005 survey period Montana received more precipitation and short-term indices were actually well above normal. Upland vegetation responded well to the added moisture, and this turned a predicted dismal year into a near-normal year for waterfowl production in northern Montana.

The portion of eastern Montana roughly south of the Missouri River (Stratum 42) had a mild winter with below-average precipitation that was a continuation of a 3-year drought affecting most of eastern Montana. However, on May 8 a significant storm system produced heavy rain and snow throughout much of stratum 42. The long-term lack of moisture in the area meant this water only slightly improved conditions for waterfowl. Some semi-permanent wetlands benefited from the precipitation and most of stratum 42 was classed as fair, with a small area of good habitat southeast of Miles City.

In the western Dakotas (strata 43-44), waterfowl production potential was largely rated fair, and poor along the border between North and South Dakota. As of May, production in these regions was expected to be below average.

In Montana and the western Dakotas, May pond counts were similar to the 2004 estimate, and 27% higher than the long-term average. Total ducks were 20% lower than both their 2004 estimate and their long-term average. Northern pintails and canvasbacks were 43% and 60% below last year's estimates, and were 73% and 39% below their long-term averages for the survey area. Mallards, American wigeon, and scaup were all similar to their 2004 estimates, and remained 23%, 39%, and 70% below their long-term averages, respectively. Green-winged teal were similar to last year's estimate, and were 113% above their long-term average for the survey area. Gadwall, northern shoveler, and blue-winged teal estimates were similar to those of 2004, and to long-term averages. The estimate for redheads did not differ from last year's, but this species remained 70% below its long-term average for the region.

Habitat conditions in the area improved markedly following May surveys. Near-record rainfall filled wetlands and brought about growth of green vegetation. The high-line region near the Canadian border even improved to "good" as of July. However, this rain likely helped only the latest nesters and their broods. Much favorable habitat was unoccupied, as many ducks likely moved elsewhere before the rains came. Average numbers of broods were observed. However, good wetland conditions should produce good brood survival, and overall production in the region should nonetheless approach average, though cold, wet weather in June may have hampered duckling survival somewhat. Overall, production potential for the survey area was considered average as of July.

Eastern Dakotas: Fall of 2004 in eastern South and North Dakota (Strata 45-49) was milder than average, with some rain in October. Wetland freeze-up did not occur in North Dakota until nearly the end of November, almost a month later than normal. By the start of the May survey, most of eastern South Dakota had received no more than 2 inches of precipitation since 1 November, and the entire state of North Dakota was 20% - 60% below its normal annual precipitation. As a result of the dry and mild winter, much of the eastern South Dakota waterfowl breeding habitat was considered poor. Temporary and seasonal wetland basins were dry on much of the drift plain, and most had been cultivated. Many dugouts and small streams were dry as well. In the southern portions of the survey area (stratum 49) and the prairie coteau (eastern stratum 48 and western stratum 49), water conditions were slightly better, and these regions were considered fair waterfowl nesting habitat. Some overflight likely occurred as the generally poor conditions offered little attraction for breeding birds to settle and establish territories. Upland nesting cover in South Dakota was poor on the drift prairie due to dry conditions and tillage through wetland basins. Nesting cover in the coteau was adequate.

Eastern North Dakota was generally in better condition than eastern South Dakota. Most of the eastern third of the North Dakota survey unit was considered fair or good habitat for nesting waterfowl. Late May rains created temporary and seasonal water and improved the condition of existing wetlands. Isolated areas of good habitat were observed around Devils Lake and in the extreme northern portion of the Missouri Coteau. The northern half of the coteau was considered fair and most of the remainder of North Dakota was poor. In North Dakota, wetland basins in the drier areas of the drift plain offered slightly better nesting cover than the drift areas of South Dakota. In all other regions of North Dakota, nesting cover was typical for each physiographic region.

May pond numbers were similar to last year's figure, and 20% below the long-term average. The total duck estimate was 14% lower than the 2004 count, but remained 10% above the long-term average. Mallard numbers were similar to those of 2004, and remained, 60% above their long-term average. Redheads and northern pintails were similar to their 2004 estimates, but were 34% and 45% below their long-term averages, respectively. Gadwall, and scaup estimates were 31% and 47% below those of 2004, but were 46% and 37% above their long-term averages, respectively. Green-winged teal counts were down 47% relative to 2004, but were similar to the long-term mean for this survey area. Northern shoveler, canvasback, blue winged teal, and American wigeon estimates were similar to last year's estimates and their long-term averages.

The eastern Dakotas received significant precipitation between May and July. In South Dakota, however, significant wetland improvements were restricted to the extreme northeastern portion of the state, with some slight improvement west of Sand Lake National Wildlife Refuge. The overall prediction for production from eastern South Dakota remained below average. In eastern North Dakota, by contrast, wetland conditions were improved over the entire survey area. Some flooding of nests may have occurred, but upland and emergent vegetation was good to excellent in many areas. Conditions in North Dakota should favor good brood survival. Overall, average waterfowl production was expected in the eastern Dakotas as of July 2005.

Northern Saskatchewan, Northern Manitoba, and Western Ontario: In northern Saskatchewan and Manitoba (strata 21-25), winter snowfall was plentiful throughout most of the region. Spring, and the accompanying ice breakup occurred relatively early across the region. As a result, many rivers, lakes and streams were high in May, which flooded vast areas of prime nesting habitat. Although breakup came early, late spring was cold and wet, which could adversely affect production. Many small beaver-pond wetlands were ideal for duck nesting; however, due to the widespread flooding, a large portion of the survey area was rated fair as of May, and the smaller remaining portion was rated good. Western Ontario (stratum 50) was also rated as good.

The total-duck estimate was 21% below the 2004 estimate, and 10% below the long-term average. The scaup estimate was 40% lower than last year's, and 41% lower than the long-term average. All other species were similar to their 2004 estimates. The green-winged teal estimate was 59% higher than the long term average for the region. American wigeon (-31%), northern shovelers (-34%), blue-winged teal (-48%), redheads (-53%), and northern pintails (-80%) were all below their long-term averages for the survey area. Mallards, gadwall, and canvasbacks were all similar to their long-term averages.

As of July, conditions were rated mostly fair, with some areas of good, throughout most of northern Saskatchewan and Northern Manitoba.

Northern Alberta, Northeastern British Columbia, and Northwest Territories: In northern Alberta, northeastern British Columbia, and the Northwest Territories (strata 13-18, 20, 75-77), conditions were fair in the center of the survey area. Northwest of Cree Lake was rated good, as was the northeastern portion of the survey area near Gillam. The southwestern corner of the survey region near Nipawin was also rated good. Heavy flooding in many regions, especially those rated fair, likely hampered nesting. Most of the survey area in northern Alberta and northeastern British Columbia (stratum 77) was fairly dry because of below-normal spring precipitation. Spring came early, with above-average temperatures in April, but a cold-snap in May delayed phenology somewhat. Water levels were low in most wetlands. Only permanent lakes and large beaver flowages had normal habitat available for waterfowl. Overall, stratum 77 was rated as fair. The Athabasca Delta (stratum 20) experienced below normal spring flooding, and was rated fair. All of the lakes surveyed had lower than normal water levels. Many of smaller associated wetlands were dry or almost dry and the normally deeper sloughs had reduced water levels. Spring was earlier than normal in the Delta, with no ice on Lake Claire.

Spring arrived earlier than normal in the southern Northwest Territories (stratum 17), and the entire stratum was rated good. All wetlands were ice free, including the mid-size and larger lakes at higher elevation on the Horn Plateau. Southern portions of the stratum had water overflowing from beaver flowages and small size ponds from recent rains. The Canadian Shield (strata 16 and 18) was rated as fair because of later than normal spring and the subsequent late ice breakup. Water levels were near or above normal in this portion of the survey area.

The Middle Mackenzie Valley (stratum 15) was rated as good due to average winter snow-melt. All mid-size and large lakes were open by June 10. The Upper Mackenzie Valley Boreal Plains/Tundra (stratum 14) experienced a slightly earlier normal spring, which provided good breeding habitat for the early nesting waterfowl species. This stratum was rated as good. Waterfowl breeding habitat was in better shape on the MacKenzie River Delta (stratum 13) than last year, although production of early-nesting species was likely tempered somewhat by the late spring in the eastern Northwest Territories portion of the survey area. Due to early ice breakup and normal water conditions, this area was rated good.

Total-duck numbers were 20% below the 2004 estimate, and 35% below the long-term average for the survey area. Mallards (-31% from 2004, -51% from long-term average), green-winged teal (-48% from 2004, -42% from long-term average), and Northern pintails (-44% from 2004, -72% from long-term average) were all below their 2004

estimates and long-term averages. American wigeon and scaup numbers were similar to 2004 counts, but remained 36% and 49% below their long-term averages, respectively. Gadwall numbers were 44% below their 2004 estimate, but remained 66% above their long-term average. Blue-winged teal, northern shovelers, redheads, and canvasbacks were all similar to last year's estimates and long-term averages.

The northernmost regions of northern Alberta and northeastern British Columbia remained very dry following May surveys. Further south, production potential as of July was rated good-very good.

Alaska, Yukon Territory, and Old Crow Flats: In Alaska, the Yukon Territory, and Old Crow Flats (strata 1-12), breeding conditions depend largely on the timing of spring phenology, because wetland conditions are less variable than on the prairies. Except for the North Slope, Alaska experienced an early spring, a weather pattern that generally favors waterfowl production. Interior Alaska was up to two weeks early, while on the western tundra phenology was approximately one week earlier than normal. Warm temperatures and heavy snowfall resulted in some flooding along many rivers, especially the Koyukuk, Innoko, and the lower Yukon. Overall, excellent to good production was anticipated following the May survey, except for flooded areas, and for the Arctic Coastal Plain, where only fair to poor production was expected.

Estimates of all duck species were similar to those of 2004, with the exception of redheads, which were 91% below their 2004 count, and 84% below their long-term average. Total duck (+45%), mallard (+101%), American wigeon (+73%), green-winged teal (+103%) and northern shoveler (+158%) estimates were all above their long-term averages. Gadwall, blue-winged teal, northern pintail, canvasback, and scaup populations all remained similar to their long-term averages.

Warm temperatures and adequate, but not excessive, moisture across much of Alaska during June and July maintained the mostly excellent conditions observed by biologists in May. Overall, little changed, and excellent production was anticipated for most of Alaska, with fair to poor conditions prevailing on the Artic Coastal Plain.

Eastern Survey Area: Breeding habitat conditions were good throughout most of the eastern U.S. and Canada (strata 51-72). Northern portions of Labrador and Quebec and all of Newfoundland were rated excellent. The western James Bay lowlands was also excellent for breeding waterfowl because of early spring phenology. Along the coast of Maine and the Maritimes, conditions were only fair for breeding waterfowl due to flooding. Habitat conditions in Maine (stratum 62) were excellent. Above-average snowfall over the winter and heavy rains in April made for full or flooded ponds and wetlands throughout the state. Significant ice was only observed on larger lakes north of Houlton. Temperatures in Maine were average during early spring, timing of ice breakup was normal and any flooding likely had minimal effects on nesting waterfowl. Habitat conditions in New Brunswick (stratum 63) were fair to good. Snowfall was average, however heavy rains in April contributed to major flooding along the St. John River and its tributaries. Wetlands, ponds and lakes were full or flooded throughout the province. Temperatures were below average during early spring, but break up was complete. Flooding reduced available habitat and may have disrupted nesting. Habitat was in excellent condition on Prince Edward Island (stratum 65). Despite heavy precipitation in April, no flooding was observed. All wetlands and ponds were full, and there was sheet water on many of the agricultural fields. Temperatures were below average during early spring, but water and habitat were plentiful, and nesting chronology appeared normal. Conditions in Newfoundland (statum 66) and Labrador (stratum 67) were excellent.

Winter precipitation and temperatures were near long-term averages across much of southern Ontario and Quebec. Spring weather was relatively mild, and precipitation was below normal, in southern Ontario, and habitats were in poor condition in the extreme southwest ranging to fair condition to the west of Toronto. Spring rains near the Bruce Peninsula and south of the Georgian Bay improved habitat conditions there, recharging many seasonal wetlands. In the hardwood-boreal transition region east of Georgian Bay and into the agricultural regions of the Ottawa River Valley around Ottawa wetland conditions were also generally good. Somewhat drier conditions were noted in the St. Lawrence lowlands of New York and little temporary or seasonal water was observed. Winter temperatures in Quebec were normal, or slightly below normal. Precipitation was below normal, except for portions of the northeast near Kuujjuaq. Agricultural regions of extreme southeastern Quebec were relatively dry with little standing water observed in agricultural drainage ditches. Wetlands were in good condition in the St. Lawrence lowlands north through Quebec City. Overall, habitat conditions were considered good

in southern Quebec, as wetland levels were adequate, though slightly below normal.

Spring melt was uncharacteristically early in northeastern Ontario in the James Bay and Hudson Bay lowlands. At the time of the survey in late May, no ice was observed on any wetlands or lakes until within 30 km of the Hudson Bay shoreline and then only the largest lakes retained residual ice cover. Good conditions for nesting waterfowl were the norm throughout Ontario.

Mergansers (-25%), mallards (-36%), American black ducks (-24%), and green-winged teal (-46%) were all below their 2004 estimates (Table 13). Ring-necked ducks and goldeneyes were similar to their 2004 estimates. None of these species differed from their long-term averages for the survey area.

As of July, habitat conditions in the Maritimes were excellent following additional precipitation in June. However, waterfowl production may have been hampered by cold wet weather. Good-very good production was expected in Quebec, where habitat remained good. Despite continued drought, good production was expected in Ontario, and above-average June temperatures brought increased plant growth. Observers reported evidence of good brood numbers in July.

Other areas: Conditions remained dry in many areas along the West Coast of the U.S. and Canada. In Washington, total mallards in the breeding population were estimated at 40,800, a small increase (2%) from last year's count, but they remained 24% below the long-term average. The estimate for total ducks (111,500) was down 13% from 2004 and 29% from the long-term average. American wigeon, green-winged teal, northern shovelers and redheads were the species whose numbers fell the most. Total duck numbers were up 5% in the wetland habitats associated the irrigation projects of the Yakima Valley and the Columbia Basin where water levels remained more stable, but the dryland habitats that depend on snowmelt to recharge potholes saw total duck reductions of 11% from 2004 and 45% from the long term average. Pothole numbers were down 41% from 2004 and 61% relative to the long-term average, the driest year since 1992.

In British Columbia, the winter of 2004-05 was characterized by a good snowpack early in winter, followed by rain and warm weather during the later part of winter. Water levels of low-elevation wetlands were higher than in 2004 but overall lower than average. Breeding habitat conditions were better than in May 2004, but remained poor overall. The total number of ducks observed in

2005 was 24% lower than in 2004 (also a drought year), and 17% below the (1988-2004) long-term average. Total diving ducks were 22% lower than in 2004 and 8% below the long-term average. Total dabbling ducks were 24% lower than in 2004 and 35% lower than the long-term average. The total number of duck breeding pairs was 11% lower than in 2004 and 22% lower than the long-term average. For diving ducks, the number of breeding pairs was 8% lower than in 2004 and 4% lower than the long-term average. The total number of dabbling duck pairs was 15% lower than in 2004 and 38% lower than the long-term average. In California, the total-duck estimate was 615,000, 49% higher than last year's estimate of 412,800, but similar to the long-term average. Mallards (318,000) were not significantly different from their 2003 estimate (262,000) or their long-term average of 372,000. In Oregon, similar trends existed for estimates of total ducks and mallards. Both were similar to 2004 estimates, but were 25% and 26% below their long-term averages, respectively.

Conditions were variable in the interior-western U.S. In Nebraska, waterfowl numbers rebounded dramatically from 2004's low numbers. Total duck numbers were up 168% to 117,100. At 81,100, the mallard count was 350% higher than the long-term average. In Nevada total duck and mallard numbers were down relative to last year. Total ducks numbered 10,700, compared to 12,000 in 2004. Only 700 mallards were counted, compared to 1,700 last year. Wyoming no longer conducts a May breeding waterfowl survey, but biologists there reported that the eastern portion of the state remains in a hydrologic drought, and many wetlands remain dry. However, there was enough precipitation this spring to improve upland nesting habitat. Overall, waterfowl production in eastern Wyoming should be poor. Most of western Wyoming has much improved wetland conditions compared to the last few years, and waterfowl production should be good.

Habitat conditions around the Great Lakes were variable. Minnesota experienced an early spring ice breakup, and an improvement in wetland conditions. Minnesota pond numbers increased 22% relative to 2004, and were similar to the 1968-2004 average. Mallard numbers (238,500) were down 36% relative to the 2004 estimate of 375,000 but still higher than the long-term average of 223,000. In Wisconsin, spring came early and was warm and dry, and wetland quality and quantity was poor. Brood habitat remained poor through June, with little rainfall in important waterfowl breeding areas. Wisconsin total duck numbers were similar to the 2004 estimate and 73% above the 1974-2004 average. Mallard

numbers were 38% higher than their 2004 level, and 81% above the long-term mean. In Michigan, wetland counts were near their 1992-2004 average, and the total duck estimate was 20% higher than last year's. Mallard numbers in Michigan (238,500) were 30% below their 2004 count, and remained 46% below the long-term average. In the Atlantic Flyway states along the East Coast of the U.S., habitat conditions were good for nesting waterfowl. Overall, normal late winter and early spring rains provided good nesting habitat. However, some areas, especially near the coast, experienced heavy rains and flooding near peak hatch, likely resulting in loss of nests and broods. Canada goose nests and broods were likely most affected by the timing of these rains and floods. Temperatures were about 10 degrees below normal across the surveyed area. In some areas, this likely caused a delay in nesting or renesting phenology. Some areas experienced drying conditions and were nearly dry by the end of May, despite good rains earlier. Total duck and mallard numbers from the Atlantic Flyway's Breeding Waterfowl survey were similar to the 2004 estimates, and to their long-term averages.

Mallard Fall-flight Index

The mid-continent mallard population is composed of mallards from the traditional survey area, and from Michigan, Minnesota, and Wisconsin. The 2005 estimate is 7.5 ± 0.3 million which is 10% lower than the 2004 estimate of 8.3 ± 0.3 million. The projected mallard fall flight index (Fig. 3), was 9.3 ± 0.1 million, similar to the 2004 estimate of 9.4 ± 0.1 million birds. These indices were based on revised mid-continent mallard population models, and therefore differ from those previously published (USFWS Adaptive Harvest Management Report 2005, Runge et al. 2002)

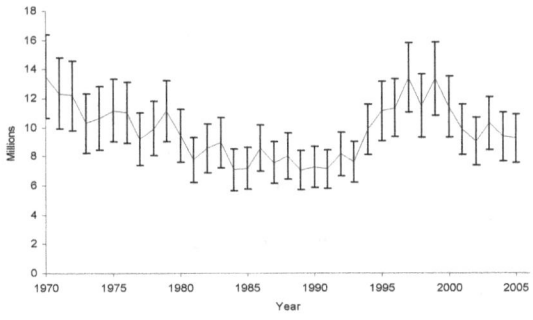

Fig. 3. Estimates and 95% confidence intervals for the size of the mallard population in the fall.

REFERENCES

Drought Watch on the Prairies, 2005. Agriculture and Agri-Food Canada. (www.agr.ca/pfra/drought.htm).

Environment Canada, 2005. Climate Trends and Variations Bulletin. Green Lane Internet Publication,Downsview,ON. (http://www.msc-smc.ec.gc.ca/ccrm/bulletin/national_e.cfm)

Link, W. A., and J. R. Sauer. 2002. A hierarchical model of population change with application to Cerulean Warblers. Ecology 83:2832-2840.

NOAA/USDA Joint Agriculture Weather Facility. 2005. Weekly Weather and Crop Bulletin. Washington, DC.(www.usda.gov/oce/waob/jawf).

Royle, J. A., W. A. Link, and J.R. Sauer. 2002. Statistical mapping of count survey data. Pages 625-638 in Predicting Species Occurances: Issues of Scale, and Accuracy (Scott, J. M., P. J. Heglund, M. L. Morrison, J. B. Haufler, M. G. Raphael, W. A. Wall, and F. B. Samson, editors). Island Press. Covello, CA, USA.

Runge, M. C., F. A. Johnson, J. A. Dubovsky, W. L. Kendall, J. Lawrence, J. Gammonley. 2002. A revised protocol for the Adaptive Harvest Management of Mid-Continent Mallards. (migratorybirds.fws.gov/reports/ahm02/MCMrevise2002.pdf)

Sauer, J.R., and S. Droege. 1990. Wood duck population trends from the North American Breeding Bird Survey. Pages 159-165 in L.H. Frederickson, G. V. Burger, S.P. Havera, D.A. Graber, R.E. Kirby, and T.S. Taylor, eds. Proceedings of the 1988 North American Wood Duck Symposium, St. Louis, MO.

U.S. Fish and Wildlife Service. 2005. Adaptive Harvest Management: 2005 Duck Hunting Season. U.S. Dept. Interior, Washington, D.C. U.S. Fish and Wildlife Service. 2005. Waterfowl Population Survey Section area reports.

Wilkins, K. A., and M. C. Otto. 2005. Trends in duck breeding populations, 1955-2005. U.S. Dept. Interior, Washington, D.C. 21pp.

STATUS OF GEESE AND SWANS

Abstract: We provide information on the population status and productivity of North American Canada geese (*Branta canadensis*), brant (*B. bernicla*), snow geese (*Chen caerulescens*), Ross' geese (*C. rossii*), emperor geese (*C. canagica*), white-fronted geese (*Anser albifrons*), and tundra swans *(Cygnus columbianus)*. The timing of spring snowmelt in important goose and swan nesting areas in most of the Arctic and subarctic was near average, or earlier than average in 2005. Delayed nesting phenology or reduced nesting effort was indicated for only Alaska's North Slope and areas of the eastern Canadian High Arctic. Primary abundance indices in 2005 increased from 2004 levels for 12 goose populations and decreased for 13 goose populations. Primary indices in 2005 increased for western tundra swans and decreased for eastern tundra swans. Of these 27 populations, the Atlantic, Eastern Prairie, Mississippi Flyway Giant, and Aleutian Canada goose populations, and the Western Arctic/Wrangel Island snow goose population displayed significant positive trends during the most recent 10-year period ($P < 0.05$). Only Short Grass Prairie Population Canada geese and Pacific brant displayed significant negative 10-year trends. The forecast for the production of geese and swans in North America in 2005 is generally favorable and improved from that of 2004.

This section summarizes information regarding the status, annual production of young, and expected fall flights of goose and tundra swan populations in North America. Information was compiled from a broad geographic area and is provided to assist managers in regulating harvest.

Most populations of geese and swans in North America nest in the Arctic or subarctic regions of Alaska and Canada (Fig. 1), but several Canada goose populations nest in temperate regions of the United States and southern Canada ("temperate-nesting" populations). The annual production of young by northern-nesting geese is influenced greatly by weather conditions on the breeding grounds, especially the timing of spring snowmelt and its impact on the initiation of nesting activity (i.e., phenology). Persistent snow cover reduces nest site availability, delays nesting activity, and often results in depressed reproductive effort and productivity. In general, goose productivity will be better than average if nesting begins by late May in western and central portions of the Arctic, and by early June in the eastern Arctic. Production usually is poor if nest initiations are delayed much beyond 15 June. For temperate-nesting Canada goose populations, recruitment rates are less variable, but productivity is influenced by localized drought and flood events.

METHODS

We have used the most widely accepted nomenclature for various waterfowl populations, but they may differ from other published information. Species nomenclature follows the List of Migratory Birds in Title 50 of the Code of Federal Regulations, Section 10.13. Some of the goose populations described herein are comprised of more than 1 subspecies and some light goose populations contain lesser snow geese and Ross' geese.

Population estimates for geese are derived from a variety of surveys conducted by biologists from federal, state, and provincial agencies, and universities (Appendices B, I, and J). Surveys include the Midwinter Survey (MWS, conducted each January in wintering areas), the Waterfowl Breeding Population and Habitat Survey (WBPHS, see Duck section of this report), surveys specifically designed for various populations, and others. When survey methodology allowed, 95% confidence intervals were presented with population estimates. The 10-year trends of population estimates were calculated through regression of the natural logarithm of survey results on year, and slope coefficients were presented and tested for equality to zero (*t*-test). Changes in population indices between the current and previous years were calculated, and, where possible, assessed with a *z*-test using the sum of sampling variances for the 2 estimates. Primary abundance indices, those related to population objectives, are described first in population-specific sections and graphed when data are available.

Because this report was completed prior to the final annual assessment of goose and swan reproduction the annual productivity of most populations can only be predicted qualitatively. Information on habitat conditions and forecasts of productivity were based primarily on information from various waterfowl surveys and interviews with field biologists. These reports provide reliable information for specific locations but may not provide accurate assessment for the vast geographic range of waterfowl populations.

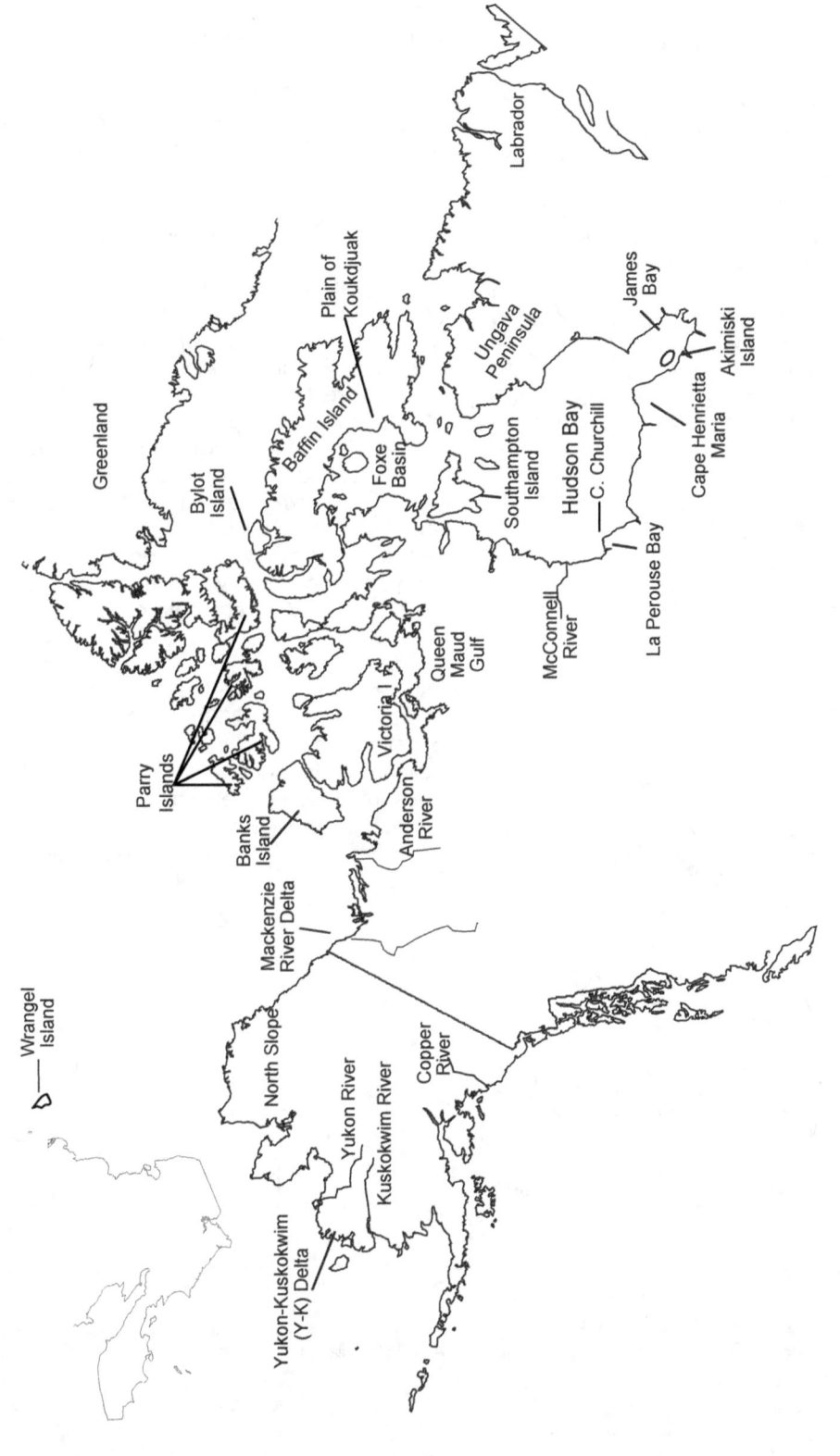

Fig. 1. Important goose nesting areas in Arctic and subarctic North America.

31

RESULTS AND DISCUSSION

Conditions in the Arctic and Subarctic

The timing of spring snowmelt in most important northern goose and swan nesting areas was near average, or earlier than average in 2005. Delayed nesting phenology or substantially reduced productivity was indicated for only Alaska's North Slope and areas of the eastern Canadian High Arctic. Conditions were exceptionally favorable on Wrangel Island, Russia and, in stark contrast to 2004, on areas around southern Hudson Bay and northern Quebec. The snow and ice cover graphic (Fig. 2, National Oceanic and Atmospheric Administration) illustrates the generally reduced snow cover across subarctic Canada in 2005 compared with 2004.

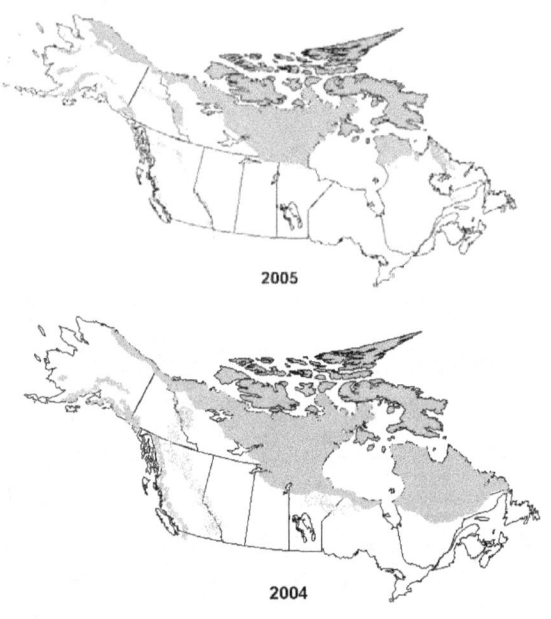

2005

2004

Fig. 2. The extent of snow and ice cover in North America on 2 June 2005 and 2 June 2004 (data from National Oceanic and Atmospheric Administration).

Conditions in Southern Canada and the United States

Conditions that influence the productivity of Canada geese vary less from year to year in these temperate regions than in the Arctic and subarctic. Given adequate wetland numbers and the absence of flood events, temperate-nesting Canada geese are reliably productive. Wetland abundance in much of this area increased in 2005, including several areas of the west that had

been gripped by drought for several years. However, in some areas (e.g., OR, UT, ND, and OH) spring rains or snows may have reduced productivity by flooding nests or decreasing the survival of goslings. Most temperate-nesting Canada goose populations likely experienced average or above average nesting conditions in 2005.

Status of Canada Geese

North Atlantic Population (NAP): NAP Canada geese principally nest in Newfoundland and Labrador. They generally commingle during winter with other Atlantic Flyway Canada geese, although NAP geese have a more coastal distribution than other populations (Fig. 3).

During the 2005 WBPHS, biologists estimated 51,300 ($\pm$ 23,100) indicated pairs (singles plus pairs) within NAP range (strata 66 and 67), 24% fewer than in 2004 (P = 0.436, Fig. 4). Indicated pair estimates have declined an average of 4% per year since surveys were initiated in 1996 (P = 0.131). The 2005 estimate of 129,900 ($\pm$ 62,800) total Canada geese was 34% lower than last year's estimate (P = 0.315). Total goose estimates have declined an average of 3% per year during 1996-2005 (P = 0.177). The pair density determined by the 2005 expanded CWS helicopter plot survey was the lowest since 1995, but clutch sizes were above average. Spring phenology was early and nesting conditions were favorable for geese in Newfoundland and Labrador in 2005. A fall flight similar to that of 2004 is expected.

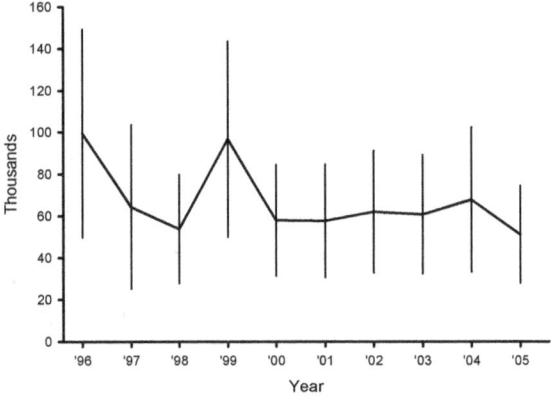

Fig. 4. Estimated number (and 95% confidence intervals) of North Atlantic Population Canada geese breeding pairs during spring.

Atlantic Population (AP): AP Canada geese nest throughout much of Quebec, especially along Ungava Bay, the eastern shore of Hudson Bay, and

32

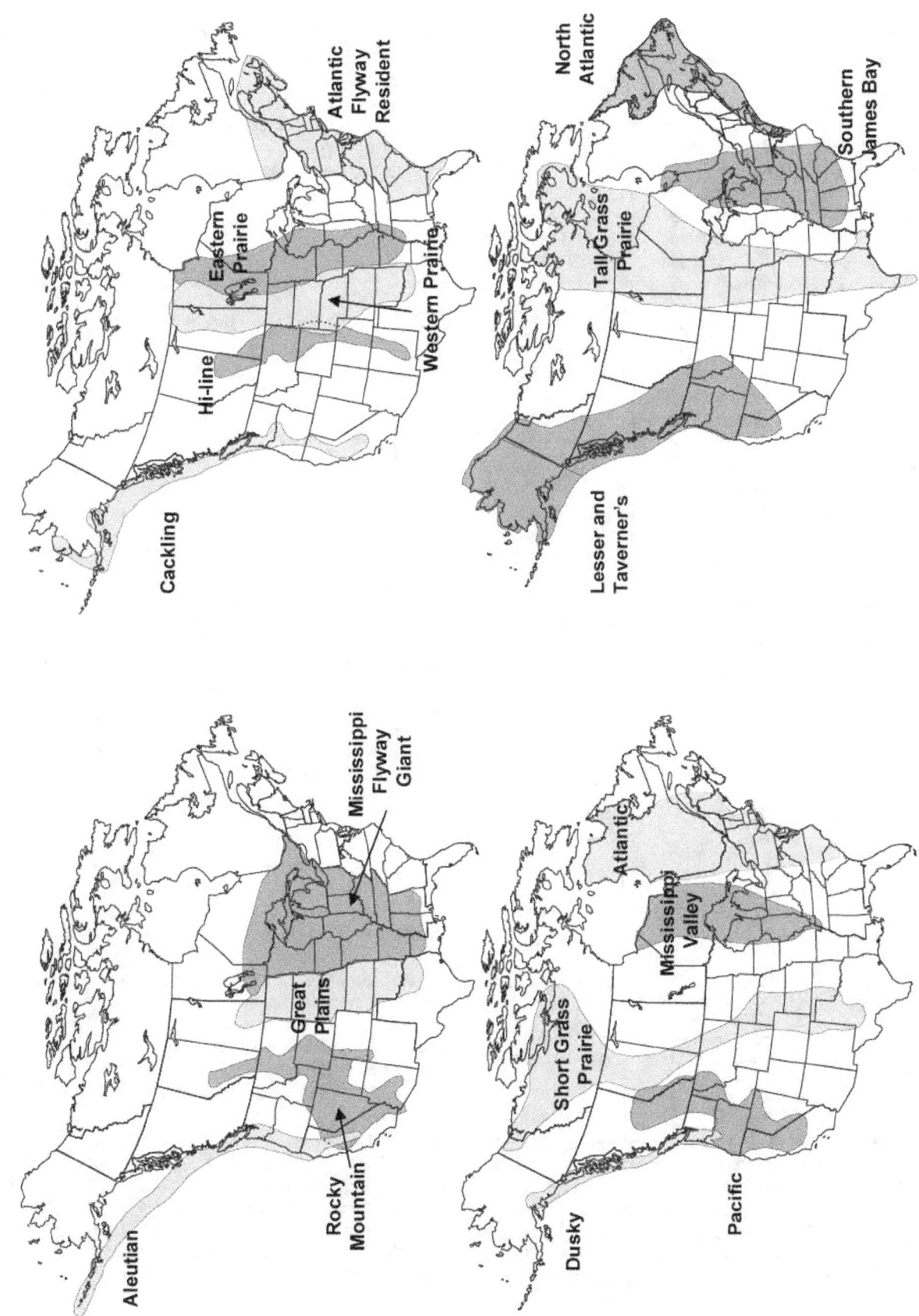

Fig. 3. Approximate ranges of Canada goose populations in North America.

on the Ungava Peninsula. The AP winters from New England to South Carolina, but the largest concentrations occur on the Delmarva Peninsula (Fig. 3).

Spring surveys in 2005 yielded an estimate of 162,400 (± 24,700) indicated breeding pairs, 7% fewer than in 2004 (P = 0.527, Fig. 5). However, survey timing in relation to hatch was slightly late this year which may have reduced detection of goose pairs. Breeding pair estimates have increased an average of 17% per year during 1996-2005 (P < 0.001). The estimated total spring population of 1,140,800 (± 177,600) geese in 2005 was 12% higher than that of last year (P = 0.312). These estimates were likely inflated by the presence of many molt migrants in 2005 and 2004. Mild spring temperatures and rapid snowmelt led to earlier than average nesting phenology in much of the AP range. The proportion of indicated pairs observed as singles (61%) was the highest recorded since 1993, suggesting an excellent nesting effort this year. The average clutch size and the number of nests found on Hudson Bay survey plots were the highest recorded since 1997. Nest success also appeared high. On Ungava Bay study areas in 2005, clutch sizes were 11% above average, nest densities were near average, nest predation rates were similar to 2004, and productivity was expected to be good. A fall flight larger than that of last year is expected.

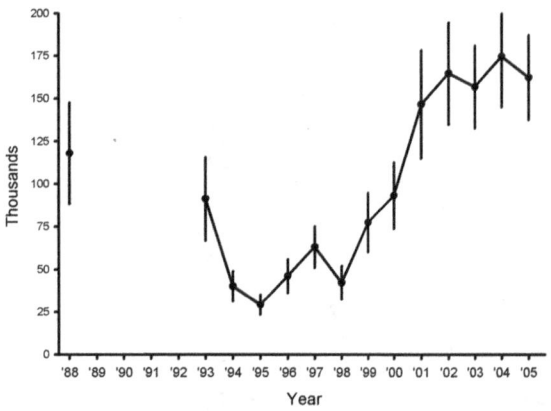

Fig. 5. Estimated number (and 95% confidence intervals) of Atlantic Population Canada goose breeding pairs in northern Quebec.

Atlantic Flyway Resident Population (AFRP): This population of large Canada geese inhabits southern Quebec, the southern Maritime provinces, and all states of the Atlantic Flyway (Fig. 3).

Surveys during spring 2005 estimated 1,064,700 (± 189,000) AFRP Canada geese in this population (Fig. 6), about 9% more than in 2004 (P = 0.523). These estimates have increased an average of 1%

per year over the last 10 years (P = 0.088). The spring of 2005 was wetter and cooler than average across AFRP states. Although some flooding occurred in northeast states, observations during banding programs indicated gosling production was at least as high as in 2004. The 2005 fall flight is expected to be similar to that of 2004.

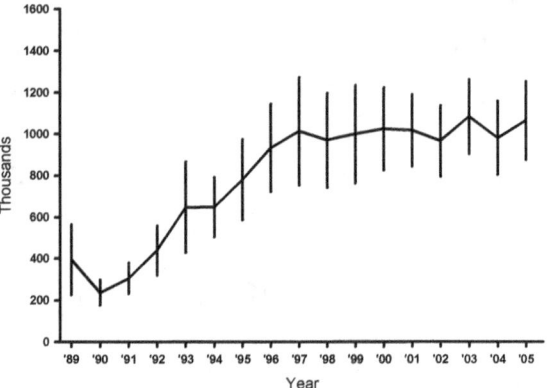

Fig. 6. Estimated number (and 95% confidence intervals) of Atlantic Flyway Resident Population Canada geese during spring.

Southern James Bay Population (SJBP): This population nests on Akimiski Island and in the Hudson Bay Lowlands to the west and south of James Bay. The SJBP winters from southern Ontario and Michigan to Mississippi, Alabama, Georgia, and South Carolina (Fig. 3).

Breeding ground surveys indicated a spring population of 46,300 (± 12,600) Canada geese in 2005, 54% lower than last year (P < 0.001, Fig. 7). These estimates have decreased an average of 6% per year since 1996 (P = 0.051). The estimate of breeding pairs in 2005 declined to 21,100 (± 6,200), 44% lower than in 2004 (P = 0.014), and a record low on Akimiski Island. However, SJBP biologists believe the survey results underestimated the population in 2005 because: 1) the late timing of surveys in relation to hatch reduced detection of nesting geese, 2) fewer than average non-breeding SJBP geese may have remained on the study area this late, and 3) use of a different survey plane which in limited comparison flights yielded lower estimates than the plane used previously. Survey biologists indicated that temperate-nesting molt migrants likely were not a factor in 2005 or 2004 surveys. Lower than average snowfall and above average late-winter temperatures contributed to a spring thaw in 2005 that was 3-4 weeks earlier than in 2004. On Akimiski Island, nesting phenology was the earliest on record since 1993. Nest density there was the highest ever recorded. Clutch sizes, and estimates of goslings leaving nests in 2005 were the highest recorded during 1993-2005. Indices of nest destruction in 2005 were 66% lower than in 2004. Although the gosling production rate of SJBP geese will be much improved over 2004, uncertainty of the breeding population precludes estimation of the fall flight.

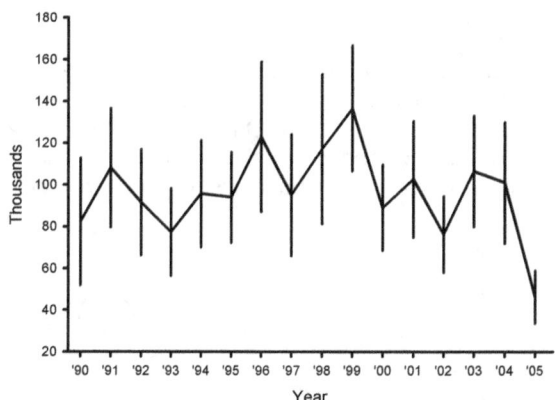

Fig. 7. Estimated total population (and 95% confidence intervals) of Southern James Bay Population Canada geese during spring.

Mississippi Valley Population (MVP): The principal nesting range of this population is in northern Ontario, especially in the Hudson Bay Lowlands, west of Hudson and James Bays. MVP Canada geese primarily concentrate during fall and winter in Wisconsin, Illinois, and Michigan (Fig. 3).

Breeding ground surveys conducted in 2005 indicated the presence of 344,900 ($\pm$ 49,200) MVP breeding adults in 2005, 25% more than in 2004 (P = 0.087). Estimates of breeding adults have declined an average of 2% per year during 1996-2005 (P = 0.242). Surveys indicated a total population of 539,300 ($\pm$ 104,400) Canada geese, a 26% decrease from 2004 (P = 0.049, Fig. 8). There is no evidence of a trend in these estimates since 1996 (P = 0.97). Molt migrant Canada geese likely had little impact on the total goose estimate this year. Biologists used a different survey plane in 2005, which in limited comparison flights yielded lower estimates than the plane used previously. Spring snowmelt occurred nearly a month earlier than in 2004 and much earlier than average. Despite snowfall in late April, nesting conditions were favorable and production is expected to be much improved over the poor production of 2004. A fall flight larger than that of 2004 is expected.

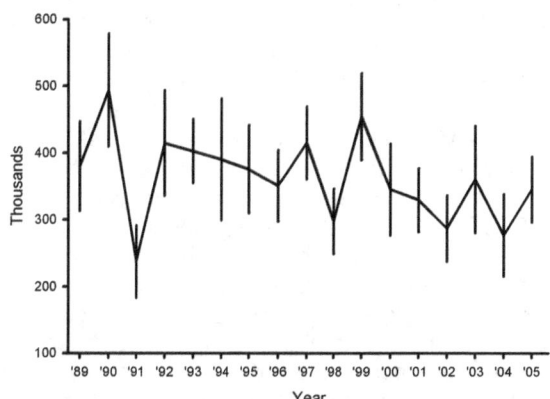

Fig. 8. Estimated number (and 95% confidence intervals) of Mississippi Valley Population breeding Canada geese during spring.

Mississippi Flyway Giant Population (MFGP): Giant Canada geese have been reestablished or introduced in all Mississippi Flyway states. This large subspecies now represents a significant portion of all Canada geese in the Mississippi Flyway (Fig. 3).

Spring surveys in 2005, yielded an estimate of 1,583,100 MFGP geese, 1% lower than the final 2004 estimate of 1,600,700 (Fig. 9). These estimates have increased an average of 5% per year since 1996 (P < 0.001). Ohio expected major nest losses due to a snowstorm in April. However, most states expected average to above average production in 2005, with especially good nesting conditions in Ontario, Michigan, and Indiana. A large fall flight, similar to that of 2004 is expected.

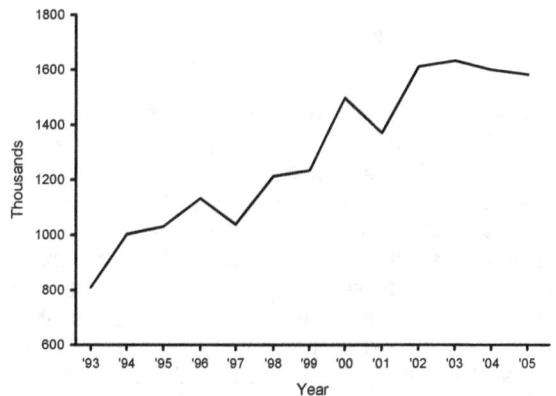

Fig. 9. Estimated number of Mississippi Flyway Giant Population Canada geese during spring.

Eastern Prairie Population (EPP): These geese nest in the Hudson Bay Lowlands of Manitoba and concentrate primarily in Manitoba, Minnesota, and Missouri during winter (Fig. 3).

35

The 2005 spring estimate of EPP geese was 254,700 (± 30,900), 12% lower than the 2004 estimate ($P = 0.142$, Fig. 10). Spring estimates have increased an average of 5% per year over the last 10 years ($P = 0.047$). The 2005 survey estimate of singles and pairs was 161,600 (± 21,100), 11% higher than last year ($P = 0.276$). These estimates have increased an average of 2% per year during 1996-2005 ($P = 0.213$). Spring phenology in 2005 was early to average in the southern portion, and near average in the northern portion of EPP range. This year, biologists on Cape Churchill observed a median hatch date of 28 June, slightly later than the long-term average (1976-2004). Nest density there was the highest since 1990, but still below the long-term mean. Mean clutch size (3.8 eggs) and the nest success index were near the long-term average. A fall flight larger than that of 2004 is expected.

included in the WBPHS was 592,100 (± 86,500), 14% lower than last year ($P = 0.204$). The WBPHS estimates have increased an average of 5% per year since 1996 ($P = 0.004$). Goose production in the WPP range likely was improved from 2004 due to earlier snowmelt and improved wetland abundance. Most states in the GPP range reported near average nesting conditions and production. However, North Dakota reported low Canada goose brood sizes there, perhaps due to cold and wet weather during the hatch period in North Dakota, a weather pattern that also occurred in Saskatchewan. A fall flight somewhat lower than that of last year is expected.

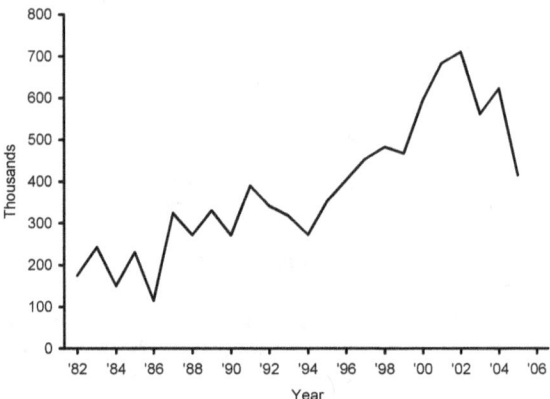

Fig. 11. Estimated number of Western Prairie Population/Great Plains Population Canada geese during winter.

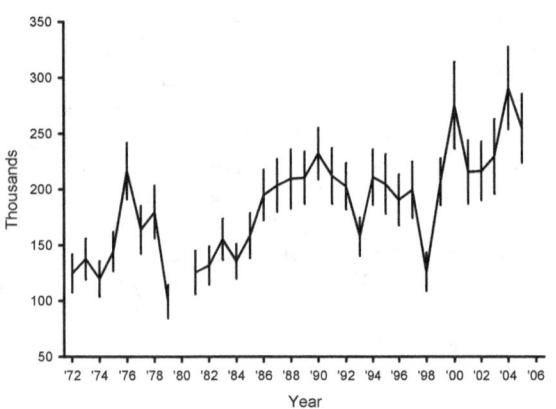

Fig. 10. Estimated number (and 95% confidence intervals) of Eastern Prairie Population Canada geese during spring.

Western Prairie and Great Plains Populations (WPP/GPP): The WPP is composed of mid-sized and large Canada geese that nest in eastern Saskatchewan and western Manitoba. The GPP is composed of large Canada geese resulting from restoration efforts in Saskatchewan, North Dakota, South Dakota, Nebraska, Kansas, Oklahoma, and Texas. Geese from these breeding populations commingle during migration with other Canada geese along the Missouri River in the Dakotas and on reservoirs from southwestern Kansas to Texas (Fig. 3). These 2 populations are managed jointly and surveyed during winter.

During the 2005 MWS, 415,100 WPP/GPP geese were counted, 33% fewer than in 2004 (Fig. 11). These indices have increased an average of 3% per year since 1996 ($P = 0.233$). In 2005, the estimated spring population in the portion of WPP/GPP range

Tall Grass Prairie Population (TGPP): These small Canada geese nest on Baffin (particularly on the Great Plain of the Koukdjuak), Southampton, and King William Islands; north of the Maguse and McConnell Rivers on the Hudson Bay coast; and in the eastern Queen Maud Gulf region. TGPP Canada geese winter mainly in Oklahoma, Texas, and northeastern Mexico (Fig. 3). These geese mix with other Canada geese on wintering areas, making it difficult to estimate the size of the winter population.

During the 2005 MWS in the Central Flyway, 400,800 TGPP geese were counted, 13% fewer than in 2004 (Fig. 12). These estimates have increased an average of 6% per year during 1996-2005 ($P = 0.229$). Biologists report that the timing of snowmelt during the spring of 2005 appeared to be earlier than average near the McConnell River Sanctuary and near average in the Queen Maud Gulf Sanctuary and Southampton Island, but appeared to have been delayed on King William and Baffin Islands by harsh weather in late May and June. Limited information suggests production of TGPP Canada geese will be similar to that of 2004.

36

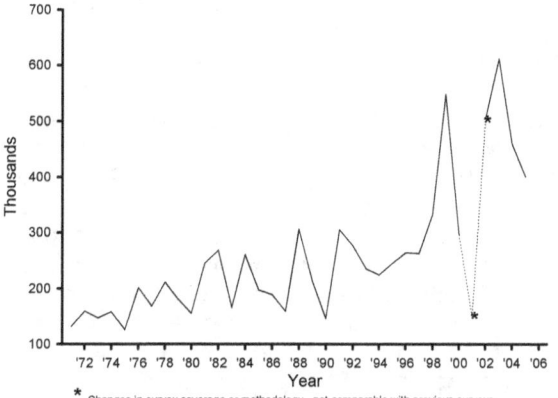

Fig. 12. Estimated number of Tall Grass Prairie Population Canada geese in the Central Flyway during winter.

Short Grass Prairie Population (SGPP): These small Canada geese nest on Victoria and Jenny Lind Islands and on the mainland from the Queen Maud Gulf west and south to the Mackenzie River and northern Alberta. These geese winter in southeastern Colorado, northeastern New Mexico, and the Oklahoma and Texas panhandles (Fig. 3).

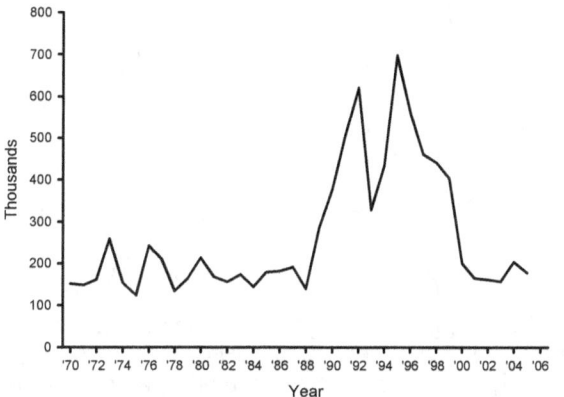

Fig. 13. Estimated number of Short Grass Prairie Population Canada geese during winter.

The MWS index of SGPP Canada geese in 2005 was 177,200, 13% lower than in 2004 (Fig. 13). These indices have declined an average of 15% per year since 1996 (P = 0.001). In 2005, the estimated spring population of SGPP geese in the Northwest Territories (WBPHS strata 13-18) was 116,700 ($\pm$ 47,400), a 20% increase from 2004 (P = 0.529). WBPHS estimates have increased an average of 3% per year since 1996 (P = 0.446). Nesting phenology of Canada geese and light geese are influenced by many of the same factors. The timing of spring snowmelt and nest initiation of light geese at Karrak Lake was near average in 2005. Surveys on Victoria

Island and the mainland of the western Canadian Arctic suggested an early snowmelt and good Canada goose nesting efforts. Additionally, wetland conditions in WBPHS strata 13-18 were considered favorable for waterfowl nesting. Although specific information is limited, production from SGPP geese is expected to be average or better in 2005.

Hi-line Population (HLP): These large Canada geese nest in southeastern Alberta, southwestern Saskatchewan, eastern Montana and Wyoming, and in Colorado. They winter in Colorado and in central New Mexico (Fig. 3).

The 2005 MWS indicated a total of 207,400 HLP Canada geese, 4% fewer than last year's estimate (Fig. 14). The MWS estimates have increased an average of 4% per year since 1996 (P = 0.145). The WBPHS yields an estimate of the HLP spring population in Saskatchewan, Alberta, and Montana. The 2005 WBPHS estimate was 236,200 ($\pm$ 49,400), 18% higher than the 2004 estimate (P = 0.320). WBPHS population estimates have increased an average of 1% per year during 1996-2005 (P = 0.530). Wyoming's estimate of the HLP breeding population there was 18,400, an increase of 16% from 2004. Wetland abundance was relatively low throughout most of HLP range at the end of last winter and into spring. Substantial rainfall occurred in May and June and improved wetland conditions, but had an unknown impact regarding nest flooding and gosling survival. The fall flight of HLP geese is expected to be similar to that of 2004.

Fig. 14. Estimated number of Hi-line Population Canada geese during winter.

Rocky Mountain Population (RMP): These large Canada geese nest in southern Alberta and western Montana, and the inter-mountain regions of Utah, Idaho, Nevada, Wyoming, and Colorado. They winter mainly in central and southern California, Arizona, Nevada, Utah, Idaho, and Montana (Fig. 3).

Spring population estimates from RMP states and provinces in 2005 totaled 172,000, 8% higher than in 2004. These estimates have increased an average of 3% per year during the last 10 years ($P = 0.091$, Fig. 15). Although southern Alberta remains dry, late winter and spring precipitation has been restoring many U.S. RMP areas that have been subjected to drought for several years. In some areas, spring rains may have flooded nests, and cold, wet weather during hatch may have reduced production in some RMP areas. Colorado and Utah expected gosling production to be reduced due to flooding. The fall flight of RMP geese is expected to be similar to that of last year.

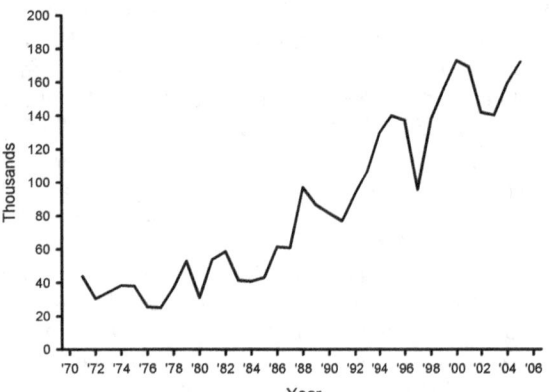

Fig. 15. Estimated number of Rocky Mountain Population Canada geese during spring.

Pacific Population (PP): These large Canada geese nest and winter west of the Rocky Mountains from northern Alberta and British Columbia south through the Pacific Northwest to California (Fig. 3).

Most PP geese are surveyed in Alberta and Oregon. In 2005, survey indices in Alberta (WBPHS strata 76-77) and Oregon were 44,400 and 41,900, respectively. These indices represent declines of 25% ($P = 0.507$) and 19%, respectively from indices in 2004. Breeding population indices declined in 3, and increased in 2 other states or provinces. California and British Columbia expected good to excellent production. Wetland conditions improved in Oregon, Montana, and Nevada due to spring rains in 2005, but the timing of rains may have reduced goose productivity there. Consolidated assessment of PP productivity or fall flight cannot be made with the available information.

Dusky Canada Geese: These mid-sized Canada geese predominantly nest on the Copper River Delta of southeastern Alaska, and winter principally in the Willamette and Lower Columbia River Valleys of Oregon and Washington (Fig. 3).

The size of the population is estimated through observations of marked geese during December and January. The 2004-2005 population estimate was 21,800 ($\pm$ 4,600), 46% higher than in 2003-2004 ($P = 0.020$, Fig. 16). These estimates have increased an average 3% per year during the last 10-year period ($P = 0.215$). Preliminary results from the 2005 spring survey of the Copper River Delta indicated the index of singles and pairs increased 47%, and total dusky Canada geese increased 58% from last year's levels. The 2005 total goose estimate exceeds the long-term average (since 1986). Increases in population indices were not unexpected in 2005, given good nest success in 3 of the 4 previous years. In 2005, the Copper River Delta experienced a warm spring, with snowmelt and nesting phenology earlier than average. However, preliminary results indicate nest success was very low this year, perhaps the lowest of the previous 9 years. A fall flight similar to that of last year is expected.

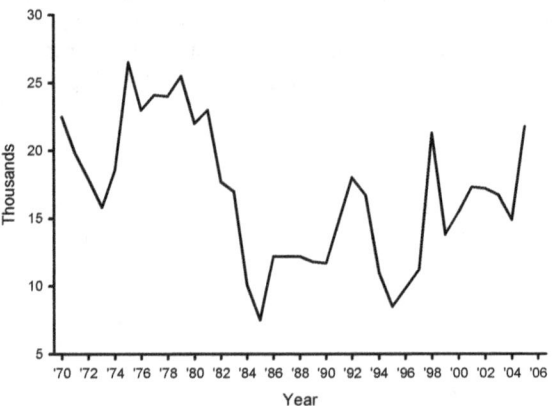

Fig. 16. Estimated number of dusky Canada geese during winter.

Cackling Canada Geese: Cackling Canada geese nest on the Yukon-Kuskokwim Delta (YKD) of western Alaska. They primarily winter in the Willamette and Lower Columbia River Valleys of Oregon and Washington (Fig. 3).

The primary index of this population was a fall estimate from 1979-1998. Since 1999, the index has been an estimate of the subsequent fall population derived from spring counts of adults on the YKD. The fall estimate for 2005 is 156,900, 21% higher than that of 2004. These estimates have decreased an average of 1% per year since 1996 ($P = 0.478$, Fig. 17). Surveys in the coastal zone of the YKD during spring 2005 indicated increased numbers of single and paired cackling geese, and an increase of 27% in total birds from 2004 estimates. Spring phenology on the YKD was about 1 week earlier than average and mean hatching date for these geese was 4 days earlier than average. YKD nesting

38

surveys indicated reductions in average clutch size and nest success from the very good year of 2004. A fall flight somewhat larger than that of last year is expected.

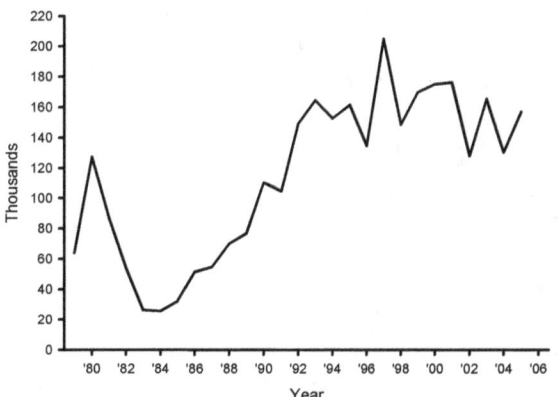

Fig. 17. Number of cackling Canada geese estimated from fall and spring surveys.

Lesser and Taverner's Canada Geese: These subspecies nest throughout much of interior and south-central Alaska and winter in Washington, Oregon, and California (Fig. 3). Taverner's geese are more associated with the North Slope and tundra areas, while lesser Canada geese tend to nest in Alaska's interior. However, these subspecies mix with other Canada geese throughout the year and reliable estimates of separate populations are not presently available.

The estimated number of Canada geese within WBPHS strata predominantly occupied by these geese (strata 1-6, 8, 10-12) in 2005 decreased 2% from 2004 levels. These estimates have declined an average of 4% per year since 1996 ($P = 0.084$). In Alaska's interior, spring breakup varied from average to 2 weeks earlier than average. The Koyukuk and other central Alaska rivers experienced widespread and prolonged flooding, and the nesting of lesser Canada geese there was redistributed but successful. Spring snowmelt on the North Slope was the latest observed in many years and production of Taverner's geese there is expected to be poor.

Aleutian Canada Geese (ACG): The Aleutian Canada goose was listed as endangered in 1967 (the population numbered approximately 800 birds in 1974) and was delisted in 2001. These geese now nest primarily on the Aleutian Islands, although historically they nested from near Kodiak Island, Alaska to the Kuril Islands in Asia. They now winter along the Pacific Coast to central California (Fig. 3).

The population estimate based on observations of neckbanded geese in California during 2004-2005 was 63,800 ($\pm$ 12,400), 9% lower than last year's record high estimate ($P = 0.555$, Fig. 18). These indirect estimates have increased an average of 12% per year over the last 10 years ($P < 0.001$). The Aleutian Islands experienced light winter snowfall and an early spring breakup again in 2005. Nesting phenology for Aleutian Canada geese was similar to 2004, which was the earliest on record. Clutch sizes were near average and another large fall flight, similar to that of 2004 is expected.

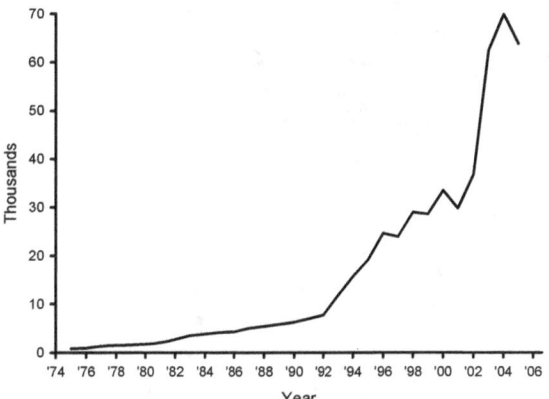

Fig. 18. Number of Aleutian Canada geese estimated from winter estimates and mark-resight methods.

Status of Light Geese

The term light geese refers to both snow geese and Ross' geese (including both white and blue color phases), and the lesser (*C. c. caerulescens*) and greater (*C. c. atlantica*) snow goose subspecies. Another collective term, mid-continent light geese, includes lesser snow and Ross' geese of 2 populations: the Mid-continent Population and the Western Central Flyway Population.

Ross' Geese: Most Ross' geese nest in the Queen Maud Gulf region, but increasing numbers nest along the western coast of Hudson Bay, and Southampton, Baffin, and Banks Islands. Ross' geese are present in the range of 3 different populations of light geese and primarily winter in California, New Mexico, Texas, and Mexico, with increasing numbers in Louisiana and Arkansas (Fig. 19).

Periodic photo-inventories and annual surveys in the Queen Maud Gulf indicate the spring Ross' goose population has increased rapidly and by 2000 had exceeded 800,000 adult geese. Comprehensive annual estimates of total population size are not available, but surveys on wintering and breeding areas indicate increases in range, number, and proportions of Ross' geese. The proportion of

39

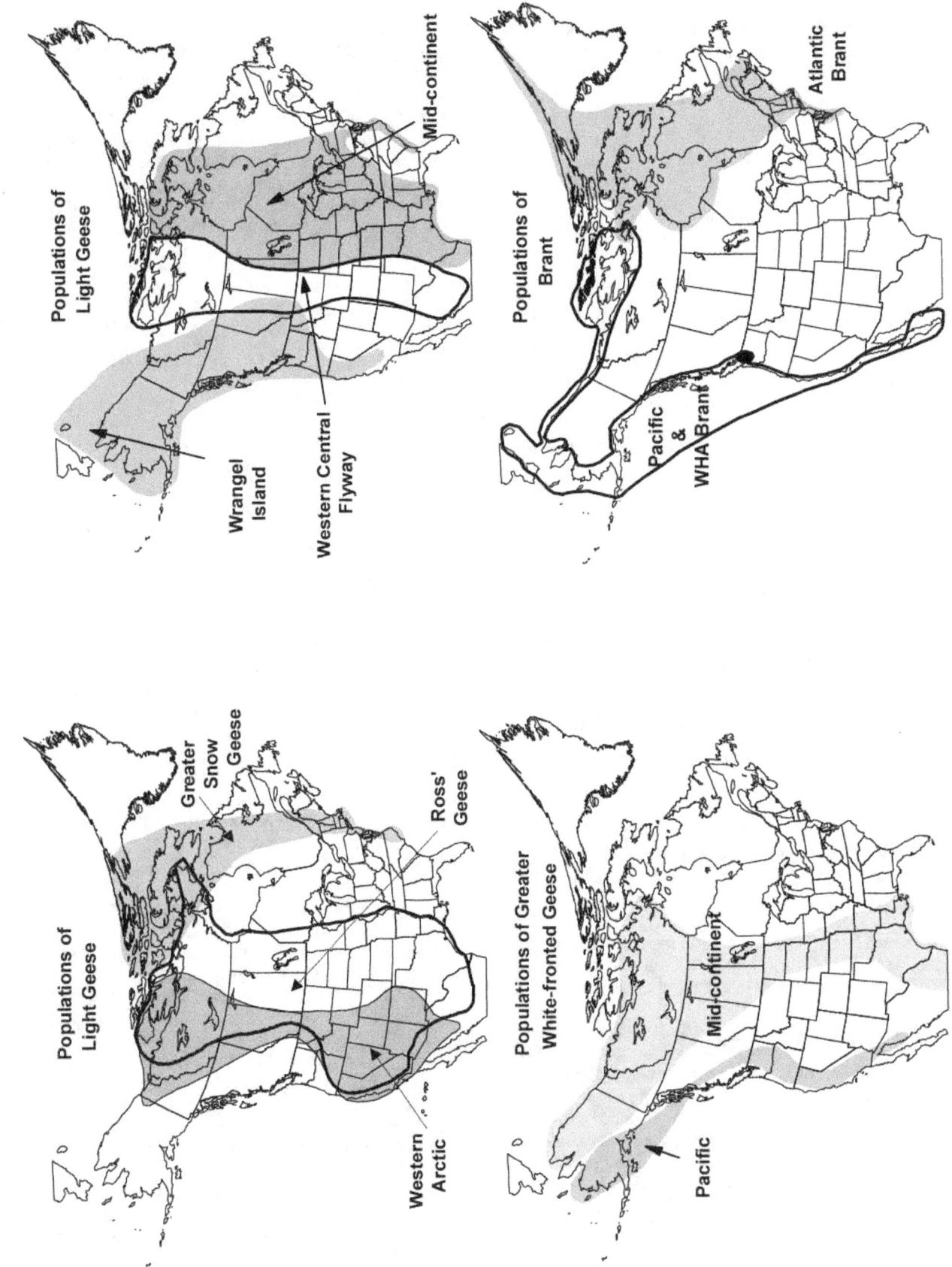

Fig. 19. Approximate ranges of brant and snow, Ross', and white-fronted goose populations in North America.

Ross' geese, assessed annually throughout the wintering range of the Western Central Flyway Population, has increased since 1984 (Fig. 20), while the total population has also increased (see Western Central Flyway Light Geese below). The largest Ross' goose colonies are near Karrak Lake in the Queen Maud Gulf. Researchers have estimated an 11% average annual growth rate of Ross' geese at Karrak Lake during 1995-2003 (433,800 adult Ross' geese there in 2003). An adjacent colony has grown to contain similar numbers of Ross' geese. The timing of snowmelt, nesting phenology, and weather during incubation at Karrak Lake was near average in 2005. Numbers of Ross' geese nesting near the McConnell River and at La Perouse Bay continued to increase in 2005. The 2005 estimate of nesting adults at the McConnell River, approaching 100,000, was approximately 12% and 25% higher than in 2004 and 2003, respectively. Spring phenology was near average in 2005; nesting ground conditions were wet due to heavy winter snowfall. Few foxes were observed and nest success appeared to be high there. Spring phenology on Southampton Island was reportedly near average. Overall, Ross' geese are expected to experience average or above average production this year. The size of the fall flight cannot be predicted without an annual index to the size of the total breeding population.

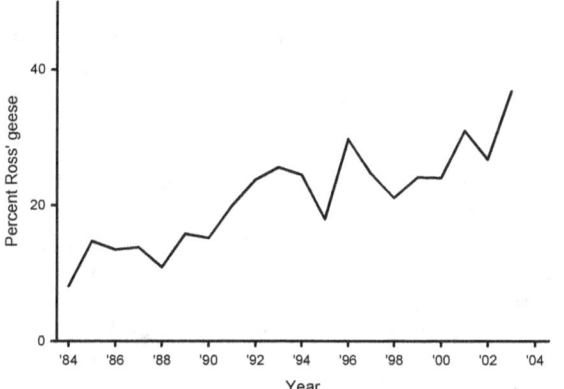

Fig. 20. Estimated proportion of Ross' geese in the Western Central Flyway Population, 1984-2004.

Mid-continent Population Light Geese (MCP): This population includes lesser snow geese and increasing numbers of Ross' geese. The MCP nest on Baffin and Southampton Islands, with smaller numbers nesting along the west coast of Hudson Bay (Fig. 19). These geese winter primarily in eastern Texas, Louisiana, and Arkansas.

During the 2005 MWS, biologists counted 2,339,400 light geese, 9% more than last year (Fig. 21, a portion of Louisiana was not surveyed in 2004).

Due to declines in these indices since 1997, the 1996-2005 data now indicate an average decline of 2% per year ($P = 0.088$). Survey biologists on Baffin Island during mid-June 2005 observed extensive snow cover and expected a reduced nesting effort there. Spring phenology was reportedly near average on Southampton Island and average production was expected. Spring phenology at Cape Henrietta Maria was earlier than average and good snow goose production is expected. At La Perouse Bay, nesting phenology was near average, but nest density in 2005 was nearly double that of the recent average. Clutch sizes were above average. However, temperatures during the incubation period had been well below average and goose forage plants had not begun above-ground growth 4 days prior to the hatching period. Biologists expressed concern about gosling survival under those conditions. Considering the potentially reduced nesting effort on Baffin Island, where most MCP geese nest, no better than average overall production is expected. However, unlike last year, migration habitats were in favorable condition in 2005, and the fall flight should be improved over that of 2004.

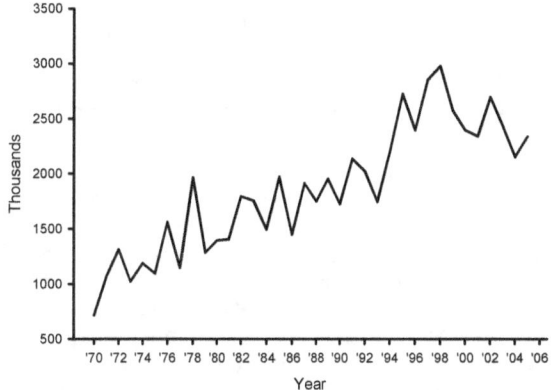

Fig. 21. Estimated number of Mid-continent Population light geese (lesser snow and Ross' geese) during winter.

Western Central Flyway Population (WCFP): This population is composed primarily of snow geese but includes a substantial proportion of Ross' geese. WCF geese nest in the central and western Canadian Arctic, with large nesting colonies near the Queen Maud Gulf and on Banks Island. These geese stage during fall in eastern Alberta and western Saskatchewan and concentrate during winter in southeastern Colorado, New Mexico, the Texas Panhandle, and the northern highlands of Mexico (Fig. 19).

WCFP geese wintering in the U.S. portion of their range are surveyed annually, but the entire range, including Mexico, is surveyed only once every 3 years. In the U.S. portion of the survey, 147,800 geese were counted in January 2005, 9% more than in 2004 (Fig. 22). This population has increased an average of 1% per year during 1996-2005 (P = 0.732). Spring snowmelt and nesting phenology were near average at Karrak Lake in the Queen Maud Gulf. Average clutch sizes from a small sample of nests in 2005 were slightly below, and equal to the 2001-2003 averages, for Ross' and snow geese, respectively. Weather during incubation at Karrak Lake was near average in 2005. Spring phenology on Banks Island was reportedly earlier than average, and Inuvialuit residents reported large numbers of nesting snow geese. Overall, production is expected to be slightly better than average for this population.

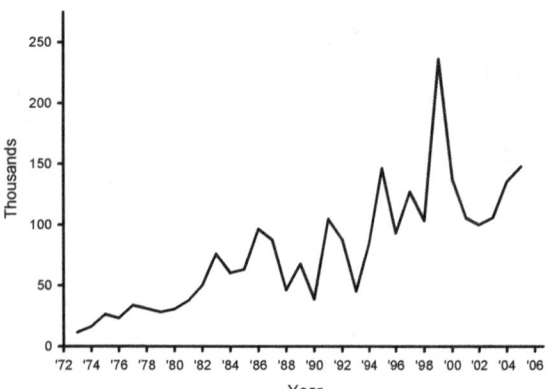

Fig. 22. Estimated number of Western Central Flyway Population light geese during winter in the United States.

Western Arctic/Wrangel Island Population (WAWI): Most of the snow geese in the Pacific Flyway originate from nesting colonies in the western and central Arctic (WA: Banks Island, the Anderson and Mackenzie River Deltas, and the western Queen Maud Gulf region) or Wrangel Island (WI), located off the northern coast of Russia. The WA segment of the population winters in central and southern California, New Mexico, and Mexico; the WI segment winters in the Puget Sound area of Washington and in northern and central California (Fig. 19). In winter, WA and WI segments commingle with light geese from other populations in California, complicating surveys.

The fall 2004 estimate of WAWI snow geese was 750,300, 28% higher than estimated in 2003 and the second highest on record (Fig. 23). Fall estimates have increased 6% per year during 1995-2004 (P = 0.026). Spring phenology on Banks Island was reportedly earlier than average, and Inuvialuit residents reported large numbers of nesting snow

geese. Surveys indicated that the nesting effort at Anderson River and Kendall Island colonies was far more extensive in 2005 than in recent years. At Wrangel Island's Tundra River colony, nesting phenology was 4-5 days earlier than average. Preliminary estimates from biologists on Wrangel Island include a spring population of 115,000-120,000, nearly 48,000 nests, a mean clutch size of 4.2 eggs, and 82% nest success. All these estimates represent increases from those of 2004 and indicate the highest level of productivity on this colony since 1970. A fall flight larger than that of last year is expected.

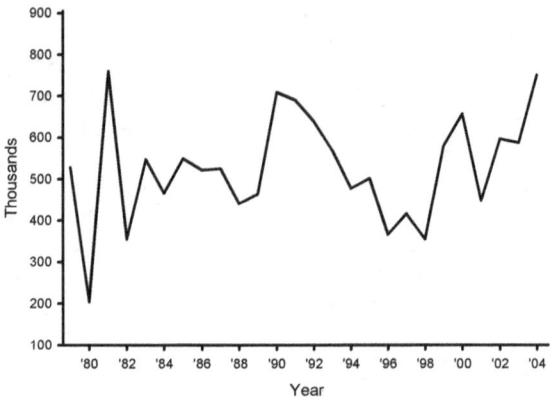

Fig. 23. Estimated number of Western Arctic/Wrangel Island Population light geese during fall.

Greater Snow Geese (GSG): This subspecies principally nests on Bylot, Axel Heiberg, Ellesmere, and Baffin Islands, and on Greenland. These geese winter along the Atlantic coast from New Jersey to North Carolina (Fig. 19).

This population is monitored on their spring staging areas near the St. Lawrence Valley in Quebec. Using 5 survey aircraft rather than 3 for the second consecutive year, the preliminary estimate from spring 2005 was 814,600 (± 115,900), 15% lower than the last year's final estimate (975,600, P = 0.15, Fig. 24). Spring estimates of greater snow geese have increased an average of 2% per year since 1996 (P = 0.299). The number of snow geese counted during the 2005 MWS in the Atlantic Flyway was 338,700, a 39% decrease from the previous survey. Midwinter counts have increased an average of 5% per year during 1996-2005 (P = 0.096). The largest known greater snow goose nesting colony is on Bylot Island. At that colony, heavy winter snowfall contributed to a delayed snowmelt and reduced goose nesting densities, although the timing of nest initiations was near average. Mean clutch size in 2005 was 3.5 eggs, slightly lower than the long-term average (3.7 eggs) and nest predation rates were moderate. A fall flight similar to or slightly lower than the long-term average is expected.

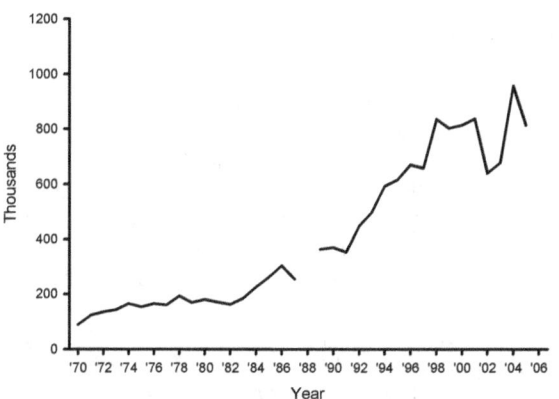

Fig. 24. Estimated number of greater snow geese during spring.

Status of Greater White-fronted Geese

Pacific Population White-fronted Geese (PP): These geese primarily nest on the Yukon-Kuskokwim Delta (YKD) of Alaska and winter in the Central Valley of California (Fig. 19).

The index for this population was a fall estimate from 1979-1998. Since 1999, the index has been a fall population estimate derived from spring surveys of adults on the YKD and Bristol Bay. The 2005 fall estimate is 443,900, 18% higher than the 2004 estimate (Fig. 25). These estimates have increased an average of 2% per year since 1996 ($P = 0.084$). Spring estimates of total white-fronted geese increased 22% in 2005 to the highest level since 1985 (146,100). Spring phenology on the YKD was about 1 week earlier than average and hatching dates for white-fronted geese were 4 days earlier than average. YKD nesting surveys indicated reductions in nest density, clutch size, and nest success from the very good year of 2004. The index of egg production was reduced 20% from 2004, but remained above the long-term average. A fall flight similar to last year's large fall flight is expected.

Mid-continent Population White-fronted Geese (MCP): These white-fronted geese nest across a broad region from central and northwestern Alaska to the central Arctic and the Foxe Basin. They concentrate in southern Saskatchewan during the fall and in Texas, Louisiana, Arkansas, and Mexico during winter (Fig. 19).

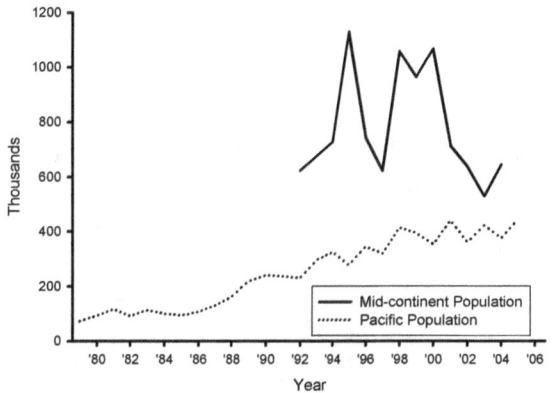

Fig. 25. Estimated number of Mid-continent and Pacific Population greater white-fronted geese during fall.

During the fall 2004 survey in Saskatchewan and Alberta, biologists counted 644,300 MCP geese, an increase of 22% from the 2003 survey (Fig. 25). During 1995-2004, these estimates have declined an average of 5% per year ($P = 0.087$). Spring phenology in MCP range varied widely in 2005. Spring phenology was near average near the Queen Maud Gulf and reportedly earlier than average in the western Canadian Arctic islands and mainland. In central Alaska, snowmelt was early but river flooding was widespread and prolonged. Production of white-fronted geese in 2005 was assessed as average or above average in all areas other than the North Slope. A fall flight somewhat larger than that of last year is expected.

Status of Brant

Atlantic Brant (ATLB): Most of this population nests on islands of the eastern Arctic. These brant winter along the Atlantic Coast from Massachusetts to North Carolina (Fig. 19).

The 2005 MWS estimate of brant in the Atlantic Flyway was 123,200, 5% lower than the 2004 estimate (Fig. 26). These estimates have increased an average of 1% per year for the most recent 10-year period ($P = 0.472$). Spring phenology was reported as near average on Southampton Island. Survey biologists on Baffin, Air Force, and King William Islands during mid-June 2005 observed extensive snow cover remaining there. Satellite imagery indicated a delayed snowmelt for additional eastern Arctic areas. Although subarctic migration habitats were in better condition in 2005 than in 2004, delayed snowmelt in portions of Atlantic brant range indicate production may be below average in 2005.

43

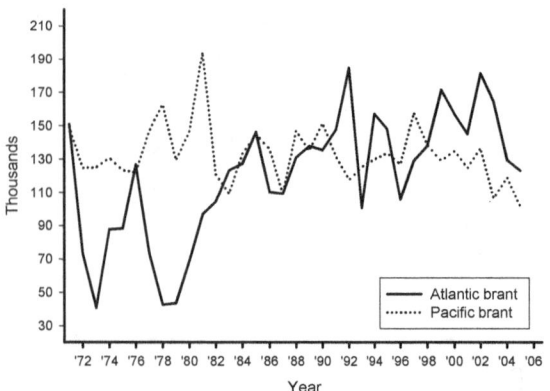

Fig. 26. Estimated number of Atlantic and Pacific Population brant during winter.

Pacific Brant (PACB): These brant nest across Alaska's Yukon-Kuskokwim Delta (YKD) and North Slope, Banks Island, other islands of the western and central Arctic, the Queen Maud Gulf, and Wrangel Island. They winter as far south as Baja California and the west coast of Mexico (Fig. 19).

The 2005 MWS estimate of brant in the Pacific Flyway and Mexico was 101,400, 15% fewer than in 2004 (Fig. 26). These estimates have decreased an average of 3% per year during 1996-2005 (P = 0.015). Spring phenology was early on the YKD, Banks and Victoria Islands, and the western Canadian mainland. Timing of goose nesting was near average near Queen Maud Gulf, but dramatically delayed on Alaska's North Slope. Brant nesting effort in 2005 increased in 4 of 5 YKD colonies compared with 2004, but nesting effort remained below the 13-year average at the 2 main colonies. At satellite colonies on the YKD, brant nest success and clutch sizes had improved from the 2004 levels. The fall flight is expected to be similar to that of last year.

Western High Arctic Brant (WHA): This population of brant nests on the Parry Islands of the Northwest Territories. The population stages in fall at Izembek Lagoon, Alaska. They predominantly winter in Padilla, Samish, and Fidalgo Bays of Washington and near Boundary Bay, British Columbia, although some individuals have been observed as far south as Mexico.

This population is monitored during the MWS in 3 Washington State counties. The 2005 MWS indicated 10,000 brant, 30% more than in 2004. These estimates have increased an average of 4% per year during 1996-2005 (P = 0.234). According to satellite imagery, most of Melville and Prince Patrick Islands remained snow covered on 30 June 2005. Similar conditions in the past resulted in <10% young in the fall flight. This suggests another poor production year for WHA brant.

Status of Emperor Geese

The breeding range of emperor geese is restricted to coastal areas of the Bering Sea, with the largest concentration on the Yukon-Kuskokwim Delta (YKD) in Alaska. Emperor geese migrate relatively short distances and primarily winter in the Aleutian Islands (Fig. 28). Since 1981, emperor geese have been surveyed annually on spring staging areas in southwestern Alaska.

The spring 2005 emperor survey estimate was 54,000 geese, 14% higher than in 2004 (Fig. 27). These estimates have declined an average of 1% per year during 1996-2005 (P = 0.754). Spring indices of breeding pairs from the YKD coastal survey were unchanged, and the total bird index declined 7% from 2004 levels. An early spring snowmelt led to emperor goose nesting phenology in 2005 about 6 days earlier than average. YKD nesting surveys indicated increased nesting effort, average clutch size, and nest success in 2005, and resulted in the second highest egg production level since 1985. A fall flight similar to the large fall flight of 2004 is expected.

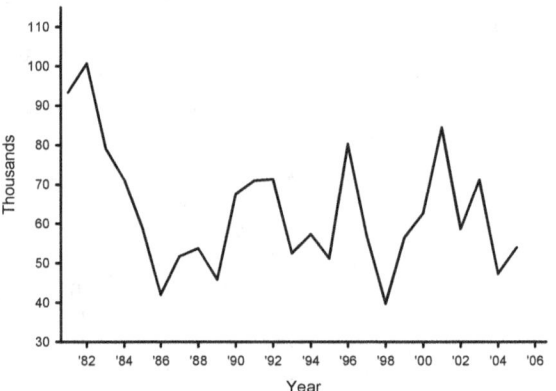

Fig. 27. Estimated numbers of emperor geese present during May surveys.

Status of Tundra Swans

Western Population Tundra Swans: These swans nest along the coastal lowlands of western Alaska, particularly between the Yukon and Kuskokwim Rivers. They winter primarily in California, Utah, and the Pacific Northwest (Fig. 28).

44

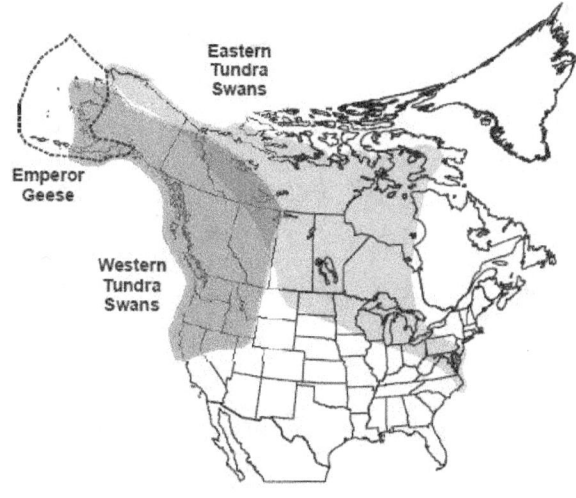

Fig. 28. Approximate range of emperor geese, and eastern and western tundra swan populations in North America.

near Baffin Island, nesting conditions in most other swan breeding areas were average or better than average in 2005. Production of eastern population tundra swans in 2005 is expected to be above average.

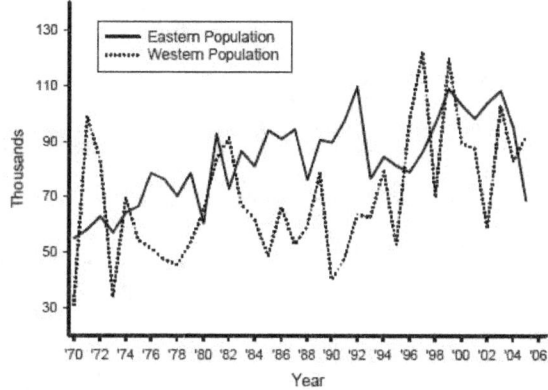

Fig. 29. Estimated numbers of Eastern and Western Population tundra swans during winter.

The 2005 MWS estimate of 92,100 swans was 11% higher than the 2004 estimate (Fig. 29). These estimates have declined an average of 2% per year during the last 10 years (P = 0.411). Spring phenology was earlier than average throughout most of western Alaska and swan nesting phenology was 3 days earlier than average on the Yukon Delta. Reduced nest density, average clutch size, and indices of nest success reduced egg production to slightly below the long-term mean there. Surveys in the coastal zone of the YKD during spring 2005 indicated substantial reductions in total swan numbers, singles and pairs, and swan nests from 2004. A fall flight somewhat smaller than that of last year is expected.

Eastern Population Tundra Swans: Eastern Population tundra swans nest from the Seward Peninsula of Alaska to the northeast shore of Hudson Bay and Baffin Island. The Mackenzie Delta and adjacent areas are of particular importance. These birds winter in coastal areas from Maryland to North Carolina (Fig. 28)

During the 2005 MWS, 68,700 eastern tundra swans were observed, 28% fewer than last year (Fig. 29). These estimates have shown no evidence of a trend during the last 10 years (P = 0.947). Surveys near the Mackenzie Delta in 2005 indicated relatively early nesting phenology, a strong nesting effort, and above average swan production. Poor tundra swan production is expected from Alaska's North Slope where nesting was delayed substantially. Although spring phenology was also delayed

45

Appendix A. Individuals that supplied information on the status of ducks.

Alaska, Yukon Territory, and Old Crow Flats (Strata 1-12): B. Conant and D. Groves

Northern Alberta, Northeastern British Columbia, and Northwest Territories (Strata 13-18, 20, and 77): C. Ferguson and J. Allen

Northern Saskatchewan and Northern Manitoba (Strata 21-24): F. Roetker and B. Fortier

Southern and Central Alberta (Strata 26-29, 75, and 76):
Air   E. Huggins and C. Pyle
Ground   P. Pryor[a], K. Froggatt[b], S. Barry[a], E. Hofman[b], M. Barr[c], N. Clements[a], J. Going[a], R. Hunka[c], T. Mathews[c], I. McFarlane[c], B. Peers[c], R. Russell[b], J. Spenst[c], S. Tucker[a], and E. Whelan[a]

Southern Saskatchewan (Strata 30-35):
Air   P. Thorpe, T. Lewis, R. King, and S. Frazer
Ground   D. Nieman[a], J. Smith[a], K.Warner[a], D. Caswell[a], J. Leafloor[a], P. Rakowski[a], M. Schuster[a], K. Dufour[a], C. Downie[a], P. Nieman[a], N. We be[a], C. Wilkinson[a], A. Williams[c], J. Caswell[a], F. Baldwin[a], C. Meuckon[a], L. Beaudoin[a], and S. Lawson[c]

Southern Manitoba (Strata 25 and 36-40):
Air   R. King and S. Frazer
Ground   D. Caswell[a], J. Leafloor[a], P. Rakowski[a], M. Schuster[a], G. Ball[b], F. Baldwin[a], L. Beaudoin[a], J. Caswell[a], J. Galbraith[a], S. Lawson[c], and C. Meuckon[a]

Montana and Western Dakotas (Strata 41-44):
Air   R. Bentley and H. Woods
Ground   K. Richkus and T. Wi kendorf

Eastern Dakotas (Strata 45-49):
Air   J. Solberg and M. Rich
Ground   P. Garrettson, K. Kruse, and E. Lang

Central Quebec (Strata 68 and 69):
Air   J. Wortham, D. Fronczak, and H. Obrecht
Helicopter D. Bordage[a], C. Lepage[a], S. Orichefsky[a], G. Gagnon[d], M. Samson[d], D. Dubé[d], J. Vallières[d]

New York, Eastern Ontario, Western James Bay Lowlands, and Southern Quebec (Strata 52-58):
Air   M. Koneff, M. Jones, and R. Raftovich
Helicopter K. Ross[a], D. McNichol[a], D. Fillman[a], B. Collins[a], and G. Ertel[d]

Central and Western Ontario (Strata 50 and 51):
Air   K. Bollinger and G. Foulks
Helicopter K. Ross[a], D. McNichol[a], D. Fillman[a], B. Collins[a], and G. Ertel[d],

Maine and Maritimes (Strata 62-67):
Air   J. Bidwell, M. Drut, and J. Goldsberry[d]
Helicopter S. Gilliland[a], P. Ryan[a], R. Hicks[a], E. Loeder[b], D. Bursey[d], G. Boyd[d], J. Myra[d], M. Paddon[d]

British Columbia: A. Breault[a], S. Jones, E. Leupin, E. McAlary, H. Gendron, G. Grigg, J. Ryder, B. Harrison, B. Arner, R. Howie, S. Wrazej, M. Wrazej, S. Helms, L. Halverson, A. Dibb, M. Dennington, K. Asquith, R. Ritcey, G. Campone, W. Haras, L. Fraser, and P. Watts[d]

California:
Air   D. Yparraguirre[b] and D. Zezulak[b]
Ground   D. Loughman[d] and J. Laughlin[d]

Michigan: S. Chadwick[b], E. Flegler[b], E. Kafcas[b], A. Karr[b], T. Maples[b], R. Matthews[d], J. Niewoonder[b], T. Reis[b], J. Robison[b], B. Scullon[b], B. Sova[b], and V. Weigold[b]

Minnesota:
Air   T. Pfingsten[b] and S. Cordts[b]
Ground   S. Kelly, W. Brininger, J. Holler, R. Papasso, T. Rondeau, S. Zodrow, K. Bousquet, L. Deede, D. Johnson, J. Kelley, B. Russell, L. Wolff, B. Bengson, M. Soler, P. Soler

Nebraska:
Air	D. Benning [d], M. Vrtiska [b], N. Lyman [d]
Ground	R. Walters [b]
Data Analysis	M. Vrtiska [b]

Nevada: K. Neill [b], J. McKelvey [b], and M. King [b]

Northeastern U.S.:
Data Analysis	R. Raftovich and M.
Connecticut	M. Huang [g], K. Kubik [b]

Delaware   Not available.

Maryland   L. Hindman[b], D. Webster[b], B. Evans[b], D. Price[b], B. Joyce[b], D. Heilmeier[b], T. DeWitt[b], T. Decker[b], G. Timko[b], K. D'Loughy[b], D. Brinker[b], R. Norris[b], R. Hill[b], R. Brown[b], P. Allen[b], and M. Mause[b]. Sergeant B. Martin[b], Natural Resources Police piloted our helicopter to complete the salt marsh plots.

Massachusetts   Massachusetts Division of Fisheries and Wildlife personnel and cooperators.

New Hampshire   T. Walski[b], J. Robinson[b], E. Orff[b], K. Bordeau[b], K. Bontaities[b], B. Ingham[b], E. Robinson[b], W. Staats[b], A. Timmins[b].

New Jersey   T. Nichols[b], J. Garris[b], J. Ziemba[b], N. Zimpfer[b], P. Castelli[b], L. Widjeskog[b], S. DeFalco[b], D. Wilkinson[b], B. Kirkpatrick[b], J. Powers[b], and S. Martka[b].

New York   Not available.

Pennsylvania   D, Brauning[b], M. J. Casalena[b], R. Coup[b], J. Dunn[b], J. Gi bert[b], I. Gregg[b], D. Gross[b], T. Hardisky[b], K. Jacobs[b], D. Koppenhaver[b], M. Lovallo[b], J. Morgan[b], B. Palmer[b], C. Rosenberry[b], M. Ternet[b], C. Thoma[b], S. Trusso[b], and J. Vreeland[b].

Rhode Island   Not available.

Vermont   D. Sausville[b], B. Crenshaw[b], J. Gobeille[b], J. Mlcuch[b], D. Blodgett[b], K. Royar[b], J. Austin[b], T. Appleton[b], J. Buck[b], and F. Hammond[b].

Virginia   T. Bidrowski [b], G. Costanzo[b], Virginia Department of Game & Inland Fisheries Staff.

Oregon: B. Bales [b], E. Miguez [b], N. Saake [b], M. Kirsch [b], M. St. Louis [b], J. Journey [b], R. Klus [b], T. Collom [b],   J. Rempel [b]

Washington: R. Friesz [b], D. Base [b], D. Volsen [b], H. Ferguson [b], P. Fowler [b], J. Tabor [b], J. Cotton [b], T. McCall [b], S. Fitkin [b], J. Heinlen [b], M. Livingston [b], J. Bernatowicz [b], W. Moore [b], E. Krausz [b], V. Brown Eagle [b], and T. Hames [b]

Wisconsin:
Air	L. Waskow [b], B. Bacon [b], P. Beringer [b], C. Cold [b], B. Glenzinski [b], and C. Milestone [b]
Ground	K. Van Horn [b], T. Bahti [b], G. Bedient [b], K. Belling [b], J. Carstens [b], N. Christel [b], M. Cipiti [b], G. Gray [b], B. Hill [b], J. Huff [b], D. Matheys [b], R. McDonough [b], K. Morgan [b], A. Oberc [b], W. Oehmichen [b], J. Robaidek [b], E. Williams [b], M. Windsor [b], D. Wyman [b], A. Kitchen, R. Krueger, R. Mockler, K. Mould, L. Nieman, B. Rudolph, J. Trick, and G. Van Vreede

Wyoming: L. Roberts [b]

We also wish to acknowledge the following individuals and groups:
The states of the Atlantic and Mississippi Flyway and Regions 3, 4, and 5 of the U.S. Fish and Wildlife Service for collecting mid-winter waterfowl survey data, from which we extract black duck counts, and J. Serie, K. Gamble, B. Raftovich, and D. Fronczak for summarizing the counts; the volunteers of the North American Breeding Bird Survey (a survey coordinated by the U.S. Geological Survey, Biological Resources Division [USGS/BRD]) for data used in estimation of wood duck population trends, and J. Sauer, USGS for conducting the wood duck trend analyses and Eastern survey data analysis. Habitat information was provided by U.S. Fish and Wildlife Service, Canadian Wildlife Service, State, and Provincial biologists.

---

[a] Canadian Wildlife Service
[b] State, Provincial, or Tribal Conservation Agency
[c] Ducks Unlimited - Canada
[d] Other organization
All others – U.S. Fish and Wildlife Service

Appendix B. Individuals that supplied information on the status of geese and swans.

Flyway-wide and Regional Survey Reports: T. Bowman, D. Caswell[a], B. Conant, K. Dickson[a], M. Drut, J. Fischer, D. Fronczak, K. Gamble, M. Koneff, K. Kruse, J. Leafloor[a], R. Oates, M. Otto, R. Raftovich, J. Serie, D. Sharp, R. Stehn, R. Trost, and G. Walters

Information from the Breeding Population and Habitat Survey: see Appendix A

North Atlantic Population of Canada Geese: J. Bidwell, and S. Gilliland[a]

Atlantic Population of Canada Geese: J. Bidwell, R. Cotter[a], W. Harvey[b], L. Hindman[b], and J. Rodrigue[a]

Atlantic Flyway Resident Population of Canada Geese: P. Castelli[b], G. Costanzo[b], W. Crenshaw, J. Dunn[b], H. Heusmann[b], L. Hindman[b], M. Huang[b], K. Jacobs[b], J. Osenkowski[b], R. Raftovich, E. Robinson[b], and T. Whittendale[b]

Southern James Bay Population of Canada Geese: K. Abraham[b], J. Hughes[a], and L. Walton[b]

Mississippi Valley Population of Canada Geese: K. Abraham[b], J. Hughes[a], and L. Walton[b]

Mississippi Flyway Population Giant Canada Geese: K. Abraham[b], D. Graber[b], J. Hopper[b], M. Gillespie[b], R. Helm[b], J. Hughes[a], D. Luukkonen[b], R. Marshalla[b], S. Maxson[b], F. McNew[b], R. Pritchert[b], M. Shieldcastle[b], K. Van Horn[b], and G. Zenner[b]

Eastern Prairie Population of Canada Geese: D. Andersen[d], M. Gillespie[b], B. Lubinski, A. Raedeke[b], M. Reiter[d], and J. Wollenberg[b]

Western Prairie and Great Plains Populations of Canada Geese: M. Johnson[b], M. Kraft[b], D. Nieman[a], M. O'Meilia[b], J. Solberg, P. Thorpe, S. Vaa[b], M. Vritiska[b]

Tall Grass Prairie Population of Canada Geese: R. Alisauskas[a], D. Caswell[a], J. Caswell[d], G. Gilchrist[a], B. Lubinski, and T. Moser

Short Grass Prairie Population of Canada Geese: R. Alisauskas[a], B. Conant, C. Ferguson, D. Graber[b], J. Hines[a], G. Raven[a], F. Roetker, and T. Moser

Hi-Line Population of Canada Geese: J. Dubovsky, J. Gammonley[b], J. Hansen[b], D. Nieman[a], L. Roberts[b], and P. Thorpe

Rocky Mountain Population of Canada Geese: T. Aldrich[b], J. Bohne[b], J. Dubovsky, C. Mortimore[b], R. Northrup[b], L. Roberts[b], T. Sanders[b], P. Thorpe, and D. Yparraguirre

Pacific Population of Canada Geese: A. Breault[a], B. Bales[b], C. Ferguson, T. Hemker[b], R. Northrup[b], D. Kraege[b], C. Mortimore[b], M. Weaver[b], and D. Yparraguirre[b]

Dusky Canada Geese: R. Anthony[d], M. Drut, B. Eldridge, T. Fondell[d], B. Larned, and T. Rothe[b]

Lesser and Taverner's Canada Geese: B. Conant, C. Dau, B. Larned, and E. Mallek

Cackling Canada Geese: M. Anthony[d], C. Dau, B. Eldridge, and M. Wege

Aleutian Canada Geese: V. Byrd

Greater Snow Geese: J. Lefebvre[a], G. Gauthier[d], and A. Reed[a]

Mid-continent Population Light Geese: K. Abraham[b], D. Caswell[a], J. Caswell[d], G. Gilchrist[a], B. Lubinski, A. Raedeke[b], J. Leafloor[a], R. Rockwell[d], L. Walton[b], and J. Wollenberg[b]

Western Central Flyway Population Light Geese: R. Alisauskas[a], J. Hines[a], P. Thorpe, and T. Moser

Appendix B. Continued.

Western Arctic/Wrangel Island Population of Lesser Snow Geese: V. Baranuk[d], S. Boyd[a], J. Hines[a], and D. Kraege[b]

Ross' Geese: R. Alisauskas[a], J. Caswell[d], J. Leafloor[a], and P. Thorpe

Pacific Population White-Fronted Geese: C. Dau, B. Eldridge, C. Ely[d], J. Fischer, and D. Groves

Mid-continent Population White-fronted Geese: R. Alisauskas[a], B. Conant, S. Durham[b], D. Groves, J. Hines[a], B. Larned, D. Lobpries[b], N. Lyman[b], E. Malleck, D. Nieman[a], F. Roetker, B. Scotton, J. Smith[a], J. Solberg, R. Walters[b], and K. Warner[a]

Pacific Brant: M. Anthony[d], B. Eldridge, and R. King

Atlantic Brant: G. Gilchrist[a], D. Caswell[a], and B. Lubinski

Western High Arctic Brant: D. Kraege[b]

Emperor Geese: C. Dau, B. Eldridge, R. King, and E. Malleck

Western Population of Tundra Swans: C. Dau and B. Eldridge

Eastern Population of Tundra Swans: C. Dau, J. Hines[a], and B. Larned

---

[a]Canadian Wildlife Service.
[b]State, Provincial, or Tribal Conservation Agency.
[c]Ducks Unlimited – Canada.
[d]Other organization.
All others - U.S. Fish and Wildlife Service.

Appendix C. Strata and transects of the Waterfowl Breeding Population and Habitat Survey.

Appendix D. Estimated number of May ponds and standard errors (in thousands) in portions of Prairie Canada and the northcentral U.S.

Year	Prairie Canada $\hat{N}$	Prairie Canada $\hat{SE}$	Northcentral U.S. [a] $\hat{N}$	Northcentral U.S. [a] $\hat{SE}$	Total $\hat{N}$	Total $\hat{SE}$
1961	1977.2	165.4				
1962	2369.1	184.6				
1963	2482.0	129.3				
1964	3370.7	173.0				
1965	4378.8	212.2				
1966	4554.5	229.3				
1967	4691.2	272.1				
1968	1985.7	120.2				
1969	3547.6	221.9				
1970	4875.0	251.2				
1971	4053.4	200.4				
1972	4009.2	250.9				
1973	2949.5	197.6				
1974	6390.1	308.3	1840.8	197.2	8230.9	366.0
1975	5320.1	271.3	1910.8	116.1	7230.9	295.1
1976	4598.8	197.1	1391.5	99.2	5990.3	220.7
1977	2277.9	120.7	771.1	51.1	3049.1	131.1
1978	3622.1	158.0	1590.4	81.7	5212.4	177.9
1979	4858.9	252.0	1522.2	70.9	6381.1	261.8
1980	2140.9	107.7	761.4	35.8	2902.3	113.5
1981	1443.0	75.3	682.8	34.0	2125.8	82.6
1982	3184.9	178.6	1458.0	86.4	4642.8	198.4
1983	3905.7	208.2	1259.2	68.7	5164.9	219.2
1984	2473.1	196.6	1766.2	90.8	4239.3	216.5
1985	4283.1	244.1	1326.9	74.0	5610.0	255.1
1986	4024.7	174.4	1734.8	74.4	5759.5	189.6
1987	2523.7	131.0	1347.8	46.8	3871.5	139.1
1988	2110.1	132.4	790.7	39.4	2900.8	138.1
1989	1692.7	89.1	1289.9	61.7	2982.7	108.4
1990	2817.3	138.3	691.2	45.9	3508.5	145.7
1991	2493.9	110.2	706.1	33.6	3200.0	115.2
1992	2783.9	141.6	825.0	30.8	3608.9	144.9
1993	2261.1	94.0	1350.6	57.1	3611.7	110.0
1994	3769.1	173.9	2215.6	88.8	5984.8	195.3
1995	3892.5	223.8	2442.9	106.8	6335.4	248.0
1996	5002.6	184.9	2479.7	135.3	7482.2	229.1
1997	5061.0	180.3	2397.2	94.4	7458.2	203.5
1998	2521.7	133.8	2065.3	89.2	4586.9	160.8
1999	3862.0	157.2	2842.3	256.8	6704.3	301.1
2000	2422.2	96.1	1524.5	99.9	3946.9	138.6
2001	2747.2	115.6	1893.2	91.5	4640.4	147.4
2002	1439.0	105.0	1281.1	63.4	2720.0	122.7
2003	3522.3	151.8	1667.8	67.4	5190.1	166.1
2004	2512.6	131.0	1407.0	101.7	3919.6	165.8
2005	3920.5	196.7	1460.7	79.7	5381.2	212.2

[a] No comparable survey data available for the northcentral U.S. during 1961-73.

Appendix E. Breeding population estimates (in thousands) for total ducks[a] and mallards for states, provinces, or regions that conduct spring surveys.

Year	British Columbia[b] Total Ducks	Mallards	California Total Ducks	Mallards	Colorado Total Ducks	Mallards	Michigan Total Ducks	Mallards	Minnesota Total Ducks	Mallards	Nebraska Total Ducks	Mallards
1955	[c]										101.5	32.0
1956											94.9	25.8
1957											154.8	26.8
1958											176.4	28.1
1959											99.7	12.1
1960					51.1	32.4					143.6	21.6
1961					58.7	32.4					141.8	43.3
1962					72.7	59.4					68.9	35.8
1963					78.0	62.1					114.9	37.4
1964					110.8	64.0					124.8	66.8
1965					111.9	60.2					52.9	20.8
1966					100.8	57.8					118.8	36.0
1967					122.2	69.7					96.2	27.6
1968					145.4	73.3			368.5	83.7	96.5	24.1
1969					138.1	57.5			345.3	88.8	100.6	26.7
1970					114.8	46.5			343.8	113.9	112.4	24.5
1971					121.4	48.3			286.9	78.5	96.0	22.3
1972					94.6	45.0			237.6	62.2	91.7	15.2
1973					112.3	45.2			415.6	99.8	85.5	19.0
1974					129.0	56.9			332.8	72.8	67.4	19.5
1975					156.7	38.2			503.3	175.8	62.6	14.8
1976					142.0	34.6			759.4	117.8	87.2	20.1
1977									536.6	134.2	152.4	24.1
1978					145.1	42.6			511.3	146.8	126.0	29.0
1979					103.2	30.9			901.4	158.7	143.8	33.6
1980					110.7	32.0			740.7	172.0	133.4	37.3
1981					188.4	36.4			515.2	154.8	66.2	19.4
1982					70.2	30.1			558.4	120.5	73.2	22.3
1983					130.6	44.2			394.2	155.8	141.6	32.2
1984					109.9	39.3			563.8	188.1	154.1	36.1
1985									580.3	216.9	75.4	28.4
1986					105.0	42.0			537.5	233.6	69.5	15.1
1987	2.7[e]	0.2			125.4	62.0			614.9	192.3	120.5	41.7
1988	4.9	0.6			123.1	63.4			752.8	271.7	126.5	27.8
1989	4.6	0.5			122.9	48.2			1021.6	273.0	136.7	18.7
1990	4.7	0.5			131.9	56.5			886.8	232.1	81.4	14.7
1991	5.9	0.6			124.1	49.8			868.2	225.0	126.3	26.0
1992	6.2	0.6	497.4	375.8	101.3	46.6	665.8	384.0	1127.3	360.9	63.4	24.4
1993	5.7	0.5	666.7	359.0	145.6	68.7	813.5	454.3	875.9	305.8	92.8	23.8
1994	6.6	0.6	483.2	311.7	141.3	68.9	848.3	440.6	1320.1	426.5	118.9	17.5
1995	6.5	0.8	589.7	368.5	123.5	54.5	812.6	559.8	912.2	319.4	142.9	42.0
1996	6.4	0.5	843.7	536.7	142.8	60.1	790.2	395.8	1062.4	314.8	132.3	38.9
1997	5.7	0.5	824.3	511.3	107.5	51.9	886.3	489.3	953.0	407.4	128.3	26.1
1998	7.3	0.9	706.8	353.9	89.1	44.8	1305.2	567.1	739.6	368.5	155.7	43.4
1999	8.5	0.9	851.0	560.1	101.0	50.2	824.8	494.3	716.5	316.4	251.2[d]	81.1
2000	8.2	0.8	562.4	347.6			1121.7	462.8	815.3	318.1	178.8	54.3
2001	7.8	0.8	413.5	302.2	26.5[f]	11.8	673.5	358.2	761.3	320.6	225.3	69.2
2002	9.0	0.6	392.0	265.3			997.3	336.8	1224.1	366.6	141.8	50.6
2003	8.6	0.6	533.7	337.1			587.2	294.1	748.9	280.5	96.7	32.9
2004	6.6	0.6	412.8	262.4			701.9	328.8	1099.3	375.3	69.9	23.2
2005	5.6	0.5	615.2	317.9			442.6	238.5	681.3	238.5	117.1	81.1

[a] Species composition for the total duck estimate varies by region.
[b] Index to waterfowl use in prime waterfowl producing areas of the province.
[c] Blanks denote that the survey was not conducted, results were not available, or survey methods changed.
[d] First year of survey after major changes in survey methodology. Hence, results from earlier years are not comparable.
[e] Survey estimates do not match those from previous reports because they have been recalculated.

Appendix E. Continued.

Year	Nevada		Northeastern US[†]		Oregon		Washington		Wisconsin	
	Total Ducks	Mallards	Total Ducks	Mallards	Total Ducks	Mallards	Total Ducks	Mallards	Total Ducks	Mallards
1955										
1956										
1957										
1958										
1959	14.2	2.1								
1960	14.1	2.1								
1961	13.5	2.0								
1962	13.8	1.7								
1963	23.8	2.2								
1964	23.5	3.0								
1965	29.3	3.5								
1966	25.7	3.4								
1967	11.4	1.5								
1968	10.5	1.2								
1969	18.2	1.4								
1970	19.6	1.5								
1971	18.3	1.1								
1972	19.0	0.9								
1973	20.7	0.7							412.7[†]	107.0
1974	17.1	0.7							435.2	94.3
1975	14.5	0.6							426.9	120.5
1976	13.6	0.6							379.5	109.9
1977	16.5	1.0							323.3	91.7
1978	11.1	0.6							271.3	61.6
1979	12.8	0.6					98.6	32.1	265.7	78.6
1980	16.6	0.9					113.7	34.1	248.1	116.5
1981	26.9	1.6					148.3	41.8	505.0	142.8
1982	21.0	1.1					146.4	49.8	218.7	89.5
1983	24.3	1.5					149.5	47.6	202.3	119.5
1984	24.0	1.4					196.3	59.3	210.0	104.8
1985	24.9	1.5					216.2	63.1	192.8	73.9
1986	26.4	1.3					203.8	60.8	262.0	110.8
1987	33.4	1.5					183.6	58.3	389.8	136.9
1988	31.7	1.3					241.8	67.2	287.1	148.9
1989	18.8	1.3					162.3	49.8	462.5	180.7
1990	22.2	1.3					168.9	56.9	328.6	151.4
1991	14.6	1.4					140.8	43.7	435.8	172.4
1992	12.4	0.9					116.3	41.0	683.8	249.7
1993	14.1	1.2	1158.1	686.6			149.8	55.0	379.4	174.5
1994	19.2	1.4	1297.3	856.3	335.6	124.1	123.9	52.7	571.2	283.4
1995	17.9	1.0	1408.5	864.1	227.3	85.3	147.3	58.9	592.4	242.2
1996	26.4	1.7	1430.9	848.6	298.0	107.8	163.3	61.6	536.3	314.4
1997	25.3	2.5	1423.5	795.2	370.3	127.3	172.8	67.0	409.3	181.0
1998	27.9	2.1	1444.0	775.2	357.0	132.3	185.3	79.0	412.8	186.9
1999	29.9	2.3	1522.7	880.0	333.4	133.1	200.2	86.2	476.6	248.4
2000	26.1	2.1	1933.5	762.6	324.0	115.9	143.6	47.7	744.4	454.0
2001	22.2	2.0	1397.4	809.4			146.4	50.5	440.1	183.5
2002	11.7	0.7	1466.2	833.7	275.3	111.7	133.3	44.7	740.8	378.5
2003	21.1	1.7	1266.2	731.9	258.7	96.9	127.8	39.8	533.5	261.3
2004	12.0	1.7	1416.9	805.9	245.0	91.9	114.9	40.0	651.5	229.2
2005	10.7	0.7	1416.2	753.6	225.3	83.0	111.5	40.8	724.3	317.2

[†] Includes all or portions of Connec icut, Delaware, Maryland, Massachusetts, New Hampshire, New Jersey, New York, Pennsylvania, Rhode Island, Vermont, and Virginia.

Appendix F. Breeding population estimates and standard errors (in thousands) for 10 species of ducks from the traditional survey area (strata 1-18, 20-50, 75-77).

	Mallard		Gadwall		American wigeon		Green-winged teal		Blue-winged teal	
Year	$\hat{N}$	$\hat{SE}$	$\hat{N}$	$\hat{SE}$	$\hat{N}$	$\hat{SE}$	$\hat{N}$	$\hat{SE}$	$\hat{N}$	$\hat{SE}$
1955	8777.3	457.1	651.5	149.5	3216.8	297.8	1807.2	291.5	5305.2	567.6
1956	10452.7	461.8	772.6	142.4	3145.0	227.8	1525.3	236.2	4997.6	527.6
1957	9296.9	443.5	666.8	148.2	2919.8	291.5	1102.9	161.2	4299.5	467.3
1958	11234.2	555.6	502.0	89.6	2551.7	177.9	1347.4	212.2	5456.6	483.7
1959	9024.3	466.6	590.0	72.7	3787.7	339.2	2653.4	459.3	5099.3	332.7
1960	7371.7	354.1	784.1	68.4	2987.6	407.0	1426.9	311.0	4293.0	294.3
1961	7330.0	510.5	654.8	77.5	3048.3	319.9	1729.3	251.5	3655.3	298.7
1962	5535.9	426.9	905.1	87.0	1958.7	145.4	722.9	117.6	3011.1	209.8
1963	6748.8	326.8	1055.3	89.5	1830.8	169.9	1242.3	226.9	3723.6	323.0
1964	6063.9	385.3	873.4	73.7	2589.6	259.7	1561.3	244.7	4020.6	320.4
1965	5131.7	274.8	1260.3	114.8	2301.1	189.4	1282.0	151.0	3594.5	270.4
1966	6731.9	311.4	1680.4	132.4	2318.4	139.2	1617.3	173.6	3733.2	233.6
1967	7509.5	338.2	1384.6	97.8	2325.5	136.2	1593.7	165.7	4491.5	305.7
1968	7089.2	340.8	1949.0	213.9	2298.6	156.1	1430.9	146.6	3462.5	389.1
1969	7531.6	280.2	1573.4	100.2	2941.4	168.6	1491.0	103.5	4138.6	239.5
1970	9985.9	617.2	1608.1	123.5	3469.9	318.5	2182.5	137.7	4861.8	372.3
1971	9416.4	459.5	1605.6	123.0	3272.9	186.2	1889.3	132.9	4610.2	322.8
1972	9265.5	363.9	1622.9	120.1	3200.1	194.1	1948.2	185.8	4278.5	230.5
1973	8079.2	377.5	1245.6	90.3	2877.9	197.4	1949.2	131.9	3332.5	220.3
1974	6880.2	351.8	1592.4	128.2	2672.0	159.3	1864.5	131.2	4976.2	394.6
1975	7726.9	344.1	1643.9	109.0	2778.3	192.0	1664.8	148.1	5885.4	337.4
1976	7933.6	337.4	1244.8	85.7	2505.2	152.7	1547.5	134.0	4744.7	294.5
1977	7397.1	381.8	1299.0	126.4	2575.1	185.9	1285.8	87.9	4462.8	328.4
1978	7425.0	307.0	1558.0	92.2	3282.4	208.0	2174.2	219.1	4498.6	293.3
1979	7883.4	327.0	1757.9	121.0	3106.5	198.2	2071.7	198.5	4875.9	297.6
1980	7706.5	307.2	1392.9	98.8	3595.5	213.2	2049.9	140.7	4895.1	295.6
1981	6409.7	308.4	1395.4	120.0	2946.0	173.0	1910.5	141.7	3720.6	242.1
1982	6408.5	302.2	1633.8	126.2	2458.7	167.3	1535.7	140.2	3657.6	203.7
1983	6456.0	286.9	1519.2	144.3	2636.2	181.4	1875.0	148.0	3366.5	197.2
1984	5415.3	258.4	1515.0	125.0	3002.2	174.2	1408.2	91.5	3979.3	267.6
1985	4960.9	234.7	1303.0	98.2	2050.7	143.7	1475.4	100.3	3502.4	246.3
1986	6124.2	241.6	1547.1	107.5	1736.5	109.9	1674.9	136.1	4478.8	237.1
1987	5789.8	217.9	1305.6	97.1	2012.5	134.3	2006.2	180.4	3528.7	220.2
1988	6369.3	310.3	1349.9	121.1	2211.1	139.1	2060.8	188.3	4011.1	290.4
1989	5645.4	244.1	1414.6	106.6	1972.9	106.0	1841.7	166.4	3125.3	229.8
1990	5452.4	238.6	1672.1	135.8	1860.1	108.3	1789.5	172.7	2776.4	178.7
1991	5444.6	205.6	1583.7	111.8	2254.0	139.5	1557.8	111.3	3763.7	270.8
1992	5976.1	241.0	2032.8	143.4	2208.4	131.9	1773.1	123.7	4333.1	263.2
1993	5708.3	208.9	1755.2	107.9	2053.0	109.3	1694.5	112.7	3192.9	205.6
1994	6980.1	282.8	2318.3	145.2	2382.2	130.3	2108.4	152.2	4616.2	259.2
1995	8269.4	287.5	2835.7	187.5	2614.5	136.3	2300.6	140.3	5140.0	253.3
1996	7941.3	262.9	2984.0	152.5	2271.7	125.4	2499.5	153.4	6407.4	353.9
1997	9939.7	308.5	3897.2	264.9	3117.6	161.6	2506.6	142.5	6124.3	330.7
1998	9640.4	301.6	3742.2	205.6	2857.7	145.3	2087.3	138.9	6398.8	332.3
1999	10805.7	344.5	3235.5	163.8	2920.1	185.5	2631.0	174.6	7149.5	364.5
2000	9470.2	290.2	3158.4	200.7	2733.1	138.8	3193.5	200.1	7431.4	425.0
2001	7904.0	226.9	2679.2	136.1	2493.5	149.6	2508.7	156.4	5757.0	288.8
2002	7503.7	246.5	2235.4	135.4	2334.4	137.9	2333.5	143.8	4206.5	227.9
2003	7949.7	267.3	2549.0	169.9	2551.4	156.9	2678.5	199.7	5518.2	312.7
2004	7425.3	282.0	2589.6	165.6	1981.3	114.9	2460.8	145.2	4073.0	238.0
2005	6755.3	280.8	2179.1	131.0	2225.1	139.2	2156.9	125.8	4585.5	236.3

Year	Northern shoveler $\hat{N}$	$\hat{SE}$	Northern pintail $\hat{N}$	$\hat{SE}$	Redhead $\hat{N}$	$\hat{SE}$	Canvasback $\hat{N}$	$\hat{SE}$	Scaup $\hat{N}$	$\hat{SE}$
1955	1642.8	218.7	9775.1	656.1	539.9	98.9	589.3	87.8	5620.1	582.1
1956	1781.4	196.4	10372.8	694.4	757.3	119.3	698.5	93.3	5994.1	434.0
1957	1476.1	181.8	6606.9	493.4	509.1	95.7	626.1	94.7	5766.9	411.7
1958	1383.8	185.1	6037.9	447.9	457.1	66.2	746.8	96.1	5350.4	355.1
1959	1577.6	301.1	5872.7	371.6	498.8	55.5	488.7	50.6	7037.6	492.3
1960	1824.5	130.1	5722.2	323.2	497.8	67.0	605.7	82.4	4868.6	362.5
1961	1383.0	166.5	4218.2	496.2	323.3	38.8	435.3	65.7	5380.0	442.2
1962	1269.0	113.9	3623.5	243.1	507.5	60.0	360.2	43.8	5286.1	426.4
1963	1398.4	143.8	3846.0	255.6	413.4	61.9	506.2	74.9	5438.4	357.9
1964	1718.3	240.3	3291.2	239.4	528.1	67.3	643.6	126.9	5131.8	386.1
1965	1423.7	114.1	3591.9	221.9	599.3	77.7	522.1	52.8	4640.0	411.2
1966	2147.0	163.9	4811.9	265.6	713.1	77.6	663.1	78.0	4439.2	356.2
1967	2314.7	154.6	5277.7	341.9	735.7	79.0	502.6	45.4	4927.7	456.1
1968	1684.5	176.8	3489.4	244.6	499.4	53.6	563.7	101.3	4412.7	351.8
1969	2156.8	117.2	5903.9	296.2	633.2	53.6	503.5	53.7	5139.8	378.5
1970	2230.4	117.4	6392.0	396.7	622.3	64.3	580.1	90.4	5662.5	391.4
1971	2011.4	122.7	5847.2	368.1	534.4	57.0	450.7	55.2	5143.3	333.8
1972	2466.5	182.8	6979.0	364.5	550.9	49.4	425.9	46.0	7997.0	718.0
1973	1619.0	112.2	4356.2	267.0	500.8	57.7	620.5	89.1	6257.4	523.1
1974	2011.3	129.9	6598.2	345.8	626.3	70.8	512.8	56.8	5780.5	409.8
1975	1980.8	106.7	5900.4	267.3	831.9	93.5	595.1	56.1	6460.0	486.0
1976	1748.1	106.9	5475.6	299.2	665.9	66.3	614.4	70.1	5818.7	348.7
1977	1451.8	82.1	3926.1	246.8	634.0	79.9	664.0	74.9	6260.2	362.8
1978	1975.3	115.6	5108.2	267.8	724.6	62.2	373.2	41.5	5984.4	403.0
1979	2406.5	135.6	5376.1	274.4	697.5	63.8	582.0	59.8	7657.9	548.6
1980	1908.2	119.9	4508.1	228.6	728.4	116.7	734.6	83.8	6381.7	421.2
1981	2333.6	177.4	3479.5	260.5	594.9	62.0	620.8	59.1	5990.9	414.2
1982	2147.6	121.7	3708.8	226.6	616.9	74.2	513.3	50.9	5532.0	380.9
1983	1875.7	105.3	3510.6	178.1	711.9	83.3	526.6	58.9	7173.8	494.9
1984	1618.2	91.9	2964.8	166.8	671.3	72.0	530.1	60.1	7024.3	484.7
1985	1702.1	125.7	2515.5	143.0	578.2	67.1	375.9	42.9	5098.0	333.1
1986	2128.2	112.0	2739.7	152.1	559.6	60.5	438.3	41.5	5235.3	355.5
1987	1950.2	118.4	2628.3	159.4	502.4	54.9	450.1	77.9	4862.7	303.8
1988	1680.9	210.4	2005.5	164.0	441.9	66.2	435.0	40.2	4671.4	309.5
1989	1538.3	95.9	2111.9	181.3	510.7	58.5	477.4	48.4	4342.1	291.3
1990	1759.3	118.6	2256.6	183.3	480.9	48.2	539.3	60.3	4293.1	264.9
1991	1716.2	104.6	1803.4	131.3	445.6	42.1	491.2	66.4	5254.9	364.9
1992	1954.4	132.1	2098.1	161.0	595.6	69.7	481.5	97.3	4639.2	291.9
1993	2046.5	114.3	2053.4	124.2	485.4	53.1	472.1	67.6	4080.1	249.4
1994	2912.0	141.4	2972.3	188.0	653.5	66.7	525.6	71.1	4529.0	253.6
1995	2854.9	150.3	2757.9	177.6	888.5	90.6	770.6	92.2	4446.4	277.6
1996	3449.0	165.7	2735.9	147.5	834.2	83.1	848.5	118.3	4217.4	234.5
1997	4120.4	194.0	3558.0	194.2	918.3	77.2	688.8	57.2	4112.3	224.2
1998	3183.2	156.5	2520.6	136.8	1005.1	122.9	685.9	63.8	3471.9	191.2
1999	3889.5	202.1	3057.9	230.5	973.4	69.5	716.0	79.1	4411.7	227.9
2000	3520.7	197.9	2907.6	170.5	926.3	78.1	706.8	81.0	4026.3	205.3
2001	3313.5	166.8	3296.0	266.6	712.0	70.2	579.8	52.7	3694.0	214.9
2002	2318.2	125.6	1789.7	125.2	564.8	69.0	486.6	43.8	3524.1	210.3
2003	3619.6	221.4	2558.2	174.8	636.8	56.6	557.6	48.0	3734.4	225.5
2004	2810.4	163.9	2184.6	155.2	605.3	51.5	617.2	64.6	3807.2	202.3
2005	3591.5	178.6	2560.5	146.8	592.3	51.7	520.6	52.9	3386.9	196.4

Appendix G. Total breeding duck estimates for the traditional survey area, in thousands.

	Traditional survey area [a]	
Year	$\hat{N}$	$\hat{SE}$
1955	39603.6	1264.0
1956	42035.2	1177.3
1957	34197.1	1016.6
1958	36528.1	1013.6
1959	40089.9	1103.6
1960	32080.5	876.8
1961	29829.0	1009.0
1962	25038.9	740.6
1963	27609.5	736.6
1964	27768.8	827.5
1965	25903.1	694.4
1966	30574.2	689.5
1967	32688.6	796.1
1968	28971.2	789.4
1969	33760.9	674.6
1970	39676.3	1008.1
1971	36905.1	821.8
1972	40748.0	987.1
1973	32573.9	805.3
1974	35422.5	819.5
1975	37792.8	836.2
1976	34342.3	707.8
1977	32049.0	743.8
1978	35505.6	745.4
1979	38622.0	843.4
1980	36224.4	737.9
1981	32267.3	734.9
1982	30784.0	678.8
1983	32635.2	725.8
1984	31004.9	716.5
1985	25638.3	574.9
1986	29092.8	609.3
1987	27412.1	562.1
1988	27361.7	660.8
1989	25112.8	555.4
1990	25079.2	539.9
1991	26605.6	588.7
1992	29417.9	605.6
1993	26312.4	493.9
1994	32523.5	598.2
1995	35869.6	629.4
1996	37753.0	779.6
1997	42556.3	718.9
1998	39081.9	652.0
1999	43435.8	733.9
2000	41838.3	740.2
2001	36177.5	633.1
2002	31181.1	547.8
2003	36225.1	664.7
2004	32164.0	579.8
2005	31734.9	555.2

[a] Total ducks in the traditional survey area include species in Appx. G plus black duck, ring-necked duck, goldeneyes, bufflehead, and ruddy duck.

Appendix H. Breeding population estimates (median, in thousands) and 95% cred bility intervals (CI) for 6 species of ducks in the eastern survey area, 1999-2005.

Year	Mergansers		Mallard		American black duck		Green-winged teal		Ring-necked duck		Goldeneyes	
	$\hat{N}$	CI	$\hat{N}$	CI	$\hat{N}$	CI	$\hat{N}$	CI	$\hat{N}$	CI	$\hat{N}$	CI
1999	602.7	(422 - 951)	554.1	(369 - 901)	1,018.0	(732 - 1,362)	627.6	(329, 1,613)	905.3	(583 - 1,560)	821.1	(449 - 2,075)
2000	653.3	(462 - 1,007)	443.8	(306 - 656)	885.9	(638 - 1,206)	347.9	(201, 771)	1,342.0	(765 - 3,241)	778.7	(424 - 2,048)
2001	636.4	(440 - 1,039)	465.0	(321 - 704)	864.9	(603 - 1,206)	265.9	(136, 761)	838.6	(562 - 1,361)	1,118.0	(566 - 3,155)
2002	1,170.0	(809 - 1,930)	517.5	(355 - 769)	1,174.0	(770 - 1,708)	588.8	(254, 2,350)	834.9	(590 - 1,267)	970.3	(507 - 2,656)
2003	890.8	(622 - 1,414)	648.1	(437 - 1,122)	976.2	(675 - 1,389)	521.1	(262, 1,571)	1,012.0	(697 - 1,550)	968.4	(495 - 2,747)
2004	995.0	(704 - 1,547)	645.5	(438 - 1,114)	1,093.0	(739 - 1,571)	775.7	(344, 2,629)	1,257.0	(839 - 2,090)	747.8	(440 - 1,587)
2005	752.8	(529 - 1,173)	411.7	(281 - 635)	826.5	(582 - 1,137)	422.9	(195, 1,256)	883.1	(572 - 1,691)	714.7	(371 - 2,078)

Appendix I. Abundance indices (in thousands) for North American Canada goose populations, 1969-2005.

Year	North Atlantic[a,b]	Atlantic[a,b]	Atlantic Flyway Resident[a]	Southern James Bay[a]	Miss. Valley[a]	Miss. Flyway Giant[a]	Eastern Prairie[a]	W. Prairie & Great Plains[c]	Tall Grass Prairie[c,g]	Short Grass Prairie[d]	Hi-line[d]	Rocky Mountain[a]	Dusky[d]	Cackling[e]	Aleutian[h]
1969/70										151.2	44.2		22.5		
1970/71									131.1	148.5	40.5	43.9	19.8		
1971/72							124.7		159.6	160.9	31.4	30.5	17.9		
1972/73							137.6		147.2	259.4	35.6	34.4	15.8		
1973/74							119.9		158.5	153.6	24.5	38.3	18.6		
1974/75							144.4		125.6	123.7	41.2	38.1	26.5		0.8
1975/76							216.5		201.5	242.5	55.6	25.4	23.0		0.9
1976/77							163.8		167.9	210.0	67.6	25.2	24.1		1.3
1977/78							179.7		211.3	134.0	65.1	37.1	24.0		1.5
1978/79							99.4		180.5	163.7	33.8	52.9	25.5	64.1	1.6
1979/80									155.2	213.0	67.3	31.0	22.0	127.4	1.7
1980/81							125.5		244.9	168.2	94.4	53.9	23.0	87.1	2.0
1981/82							131.8	175.0	268.6	156.0	81.9	58.7	17.7	54.1	2.7
1982/83							155.1	242.0	165.5	173.2	75.9	41.5	17.0	26.2	3.5
1983/84							135.6	150.0	260.7	143.5	39.5	40.8	10.1	25.8	3.8
1984/85							158.4	230.0	197.3	179.1	76.4	43.2	7.5	32.1	4.2
1985/86							194.8	115.0	189.4	181.0	69.8	61.3	12.2	51.4	4.3
1986/87							203.2	324.0	159.0	190.9	98.1	60.7		54.8	5.0
1987/88		118.0					209.2	272.1	306.1	139.1	66.8	96.8	12.2	69.9	5.4
1988/89			396.0		380.0		210.2	330.3	213.0	284.8	100.1	86.6	11.8	76.8	5.8
1989/90			236.6	82.4	494.0		231.8	271.0	146.5	378.1	105.9	81.7	11.7	110.2	6.3
1990/91			305.7	108.1	237.0		211.8	390.0	305.1	508.5	116.6	76.9		104.6	7.0
1991/92			439.2	91.6	414.2		202.5	341.9	276.3	620.2	140.5	93.3	18.0	149.3	7.7
1992/93		91.3	647.4	77.3	402.4	810.9	157.5	318.0	235.3	328.2	118.5	106.4	16.7	164.3	11.7
1993/94		40.1	648.3	95.7	390.0	1002.9	210.8	272.5	224.2	434.1	164.3	129.5	11.0	152.5	15.7
1994/95		29.3	780.0	94.0	375.3	1030.6	204.6	352.5	245.0	697.8	174.4	139.9	8.5	161.4	19.2
1995/96	99.6	46.1	932.6	123.0	350.5	1132.4	190.4	403.3	264.0	561.2	167.5	137.3		134.6	24.6
1996/97	64.4	63.2	1013.3	95.1	414.7	1038.7	199.3	453.4	262.9	460.7	148.5	95.7	11.2[h]	205.1	24.0
1997/98	53.9	42.2	970.1	117.1	297.5	1212.7	125.9	482.3	331.8	440.6	191.0	137.7	21.3[h]	148.6	29.0
1998/99	96.8	77.5	999.5	136.6	454.0	1234.1	206.7	467.2	548.2	403.2	119.5	156.2	13.8[h]	169.6	28.6
1999/00	58.0	93.2	1024.5	89.1	345.0	1497.4	275.1	594.7	295.7	200.0	270.7	172.9	15.5[h]	175.0	33.5
2000/01	57.8	146.7	1017.2	102.7	329.0	1371.3	215.4	682.7	149.1	164.1	252.9	168.9	17.3[h]	176.2	29.8
2001/02	62.0	164.8	966.0	76.3	286.5	1612.3	216.3	710.3	504.7	160.9	217.1	141.8	17.2[h]	127.9	36.8
2002/03	60.8	156.9	1083.2	106.5	360.1	1635.0	229.2	561.0	611.9	156.7	205.9	140.4	16.7[h]	165.2	62.4
2003/04	67.8	174.8	980.4	101.0	276.3	1600.7	290.7	622.1	458.7	203.6	215.6	159.2	14.9[h]	130.2	69.9
2004/05	51.3	162.4	1064.7	46.3	344.9	1583.1	254.7	415.1	400.8	177.2	207.4	172.0	21.8[h]	156.9	63.8

Canada goose population

[a] Surveys conducted in spring.
[b] Number of breeding pairs.
[c] Surveys conducted in December until 1998; in 1999 a January survey replaced the December count.
[d] Surveys conducted in January.
[e] Surveys conducted in fall through 1998; from 1999 to present a fall index is predicted from breeding ground surveys (total indicated pairs).
[f] Survey incomplete.
[g] Only Tall Grass Prairie Population geese counted in Central Flyway range are included.
[h] Indirect or preliminary estimate.

Appendix J. Abundance indices (in thousands) for light goose, greater white-fronted goose, brant, emperor goose, and tundra swan populations during 1969-2005.

Year	Light geese				White-fronted geese		Brant			Emperor geese[a]	Tundra swans	
	Greater snow geese[a]	Mid-continent[b]	Western Central Flyway[c]	Western Arctic & Wrangel[d]	Mid-continent[d]	Pacific[e]	Atlantic[c]	Pacific[c,f]	Western high Arctic[c]		Western[c]	Eastern[c]
1969/70	89.6	717.0						141.7	5.1		31.0	55.0
1970/71	123.3	1070.1					151.0	149.2	8.1		98.8	58.2
1971/72	134.8	1313.4					73.2	124.8	3.0		82.8	62.8
1972/73	143.0	1025.3	11.6				40.8	125.0	2.7		33.9	57.1
1973/74	165.0	1189.8	16.2				87.7	130.7	2.7		69.7	64.2
1974/75	153.8	1096.6	26.4				88.4	123.4	3.7		54.3	66.6
1975/76	165.6	1562.4	23.2				127.0	122.0	5.0		51.4	78.6
1976/77	160.0	1150.3	33.6				73.6	147.0	10.9		47.3	76.2
1977/78	192.6	1966.4	31.1				42.8	162.9	11.4		45.6	70.2
1978/79	170.1	1285.7	28.2	528.1		73.1	43.5	129.4	3.2		53.5	78.6
1979/80	180.0	1398.1	30.5	204.2		93.5	69.2	146.4	5.1		65.2	60.4
1980/81	170.8	1406.7	37.6	759.9		116.5	97.0	194.2	8.1	93.3	83.6	92.8
1981/82	163.0	1794.0	50.0	354.1		91.7	104.5	121.0	4.0	100.6	91.3	72.9
1982/83	185.0	1755.4	76.1	547.6		112.9	123.5	109.3	2.1	79.2	67.3	86.5
1983/84	225.4	1494.5	60.1	466.3		100.2	127.3	133.4	5.1	71.2	61.9	81.1
1984/85	260.0	1973.0	63.0	549.8		93.8	146.3	144.8	808	58.8	48.8	93.9
1985/86	303.5	1449.3	96.6	521.7		107.1	110.4	136.2	9.4	42.0	66.2	90.9
1986/87	255.0	1913.8	87.6	525.3		130.6	109.4	108.9	10.4	51.7	52.8	94.4
1987/88		1750.5	46.2			161.5	131.2	147.0	15.3	53.8	59.2	76.2
1988/89	363.2	1956.1	67.6	441.0		218.8	138.0	135.2	14.3	45.8	78.7	90.6
1989/90	368.3	1724.3	38.6	463.9		240.8	135.4	151.6	10.5	67.6	40.1	89.7
1990/91	352.6	2135.8	104.6	708.5		236.5	147.7	131.7	12.2	71.0	47.6	97.4
1991/92	448.1	2021.9	87.8	690.1		230.9	184.8	117.7	9.5	71.3	63.7	109.8
1992/93	498.4	1744.2	45.1	639.3	622.9	295.1	100.6	124.4	10.8	52.5	62.6[g]	76.6
1993/94	591.4	2200.8	84.9	569.2	676.3	324.8	157.2	130.0	11.2	57.3	79.4	84.5
1994/95	616.6	2725.1	146.4	478.2	727.3	277.5	148.2	133.7	16.9	51.2	52.9[g]	81.3
1995/96	669.1	2398.1	93.1	501.9	1129.4	344.1	105.9	126.9	4.9	80.3	98.1	79.0
1996/97	657.5	2850.9	127.2	366.3	742.5	319.0	129.1	157.9	6.0	57.1	122.5	86.1
1997/98	836.6	2977.2	103.5	416.4	622.2	413.1	138.0	138.4	6.3	39.7	70.5	96.6
1998/99	803.4	2575.7	236.4	354.3	1058.3	393.4	171.6	129.2	9.2	54.6	119.8	109.0
1999/00	813.9	2397.3	137.5	579.0	963.1	352.7	157.2	135.0	7.9	62.6	89.6	103.1
2000/01	837.4	2341.3	105.8	656.8	1067.6	438.9	145.3	124.7	4.9	84.4	87.3	98.2
2001/02	639.3	2696.1	99.9	448.1	712.3	359.7	181.6	136.7	9.0	58.7	58.7	103.8
2002/03	678.0	2435.0	105.9	596.9	637.2	422.0	164.5	106.5	4.9	71.2	102.7	108.2
2003/04	957.6	2154.1[g]	135.3	587.8	528.2	374.9	129.6	119.2	7.7	47.4	83.0	95.0
2004/05	814.6	2339.4	147.8	750.3	644.3	443.9	123.2	101.4	10.0	54.0	92.1	68.7

[a] Surveys conducted in spring.
[b] Surveys conducted in December until 1997/98; surveys since 1998/99 were conducted in January.
[c] Surveys conducted in January.
[d] Surveys conducted in autumn.
[e] Surveys conducted in fall through 1998; from 1999 to present a fall index is predicted from breeding ground surveys (total indicated birds).
[f] Beginning in 1986, counts of brant in Alaska were included with remainder of Flyway.
[g] Survey was incomplete.